The
Office Professional's
Quick
Reference
Handbook

Sheryl Lindsell-Roberts

Macmillan USA

Fourth Edition

Macmillan General Reference
A Prentice Hall Macmillan Company
15 Columbus Circle
New York, NY 10023

An Arco Book

MACMILLAN is a registered trademark of Macmillan, Inc.
ARCO is a registered trademark of Prentice-Hall, Inc.

Prior editions of this book were published under the title
The Secretary's Quick Reference Handbook.

Library of Congress Cataloging-in-Publication Data
Lindsell-Roberts, Sheryl.
   The office professional's quick reference handbook / Sheryl
Lindsell-Roberts.—4th ed.
     p. cm.
   t head of title: ARCO.
   v. ed. of: The secretary's quick reference handbook. 3rd ed.
   2.
      Arco book"—Verso t. p.
      0–02–860027–4
      retaries—Handbooks, manuals, etc. 2. Office practice—
      s, manuals, etc. I. Lindsell-Roberts, Sheryl.
      quick reference handbook. II. Title.
      5 1995
      20   94-32827
                                                              CIP

        the United States of America

            4   3   2   1

CONTENTS

Part I: Mechanics of English

Part II: Communication Techniques and Procedures

Part III: Electronic Office Technology

Part I.
Mechanics of English

CHAPTER 1

PUNCTUATION

*Commas, Semicolons, Colons, Dashes, Paren-
theses, Brackets, Underscores, Quotation Marks,
Ellipses, Periods, Question Marks, Exclamation
Points, Apostrophes, Asterisks, Diagonals or
Slashes*

Execution; impossible to be sent to Siberia.
Execution impossible; to be sent to Siberia.

If you will note the difference in meaning between the two
sentences above, you will realize the vital role punctuation
plays in communicating clear and accurate messages. The following guidelines will clarify many of the punctuation problems with which you may be having difficulty.

Commas

The comma (,) is the most misused mark of punctuation.
Its main purpose is to help the reader properly interpret the
meaning of a sentence.

ADDRESSES AND DATES

Use commas between items in an address or date.

> We are moving our headquarters to 24 Besen Parkway, New York, New York, next month. (If the ZIP code were used in this example, a comma would not be placed after the state but would follow the ZIP.)
> On Sunday, August 15, 19XX, Marc will be seventeen.

When using the month and year only, either surround the year with commas or omit them completely.

> In August, 19XX, Marc will be seventeen.
> In August 19XX Marc will be seventeen.

APPOSITIVES

Use commas to set off expressions that explain the preceding word, name, or phrase.

> Lafayette Avenue, our town's main street, is closed for repair.
> Mr. Weston, our representative, is waiting to see you.
> Mr. Weston, of Harkness Brothers, is waiting to see you.
> My only sister, Susan, has been accepted at West Point.

CONJUNCTIONS

Use a comma before a conjunction (*and, but, for, or, nor, yet*) provided the conjunction joins two independent clauses that could otherwise be complete sentences.

George will not be here at ten but will arrive at
   eleven. (independent and dependent)
George will not be here at ten, but he will arrive at
   eleven. (independent and independent)

DIRECT ADDRESS

Use commas to set off words that directly address the person
to whom you are speaking either by name, title, or relationship.

Mr. Green, please send me a copy of that letter.
Please send me a copy of that letter, Mr. Green.
Let me tell you, fellow members, what the committee
   has done.

INTRODUCTORY CLAUSES

Use a comma after an introductory clause. Note that an
introductory clause will always be followed by what could be
a complete sentence. (Some key words are *if, since, because,
when, while, as, unless, provided, after,* and *before.*)

When we finish the chapter, we will have a test.
Because you came late, you will have to stay late.
Unless you call, I will assume you are coming.
If I hear from him, I will notify you.

Use a comma to set off an independent introductory expression that serves as an interjection.

No, I do not think he is correct.
In fact, I do not think anyone knows the answer.
You know, he may have been too shy to ask.

NONRESTRICTIVE AND RESTRICTIVE ELEMENTS

Use commas to set off expressions that if omitted would not change or destroy the meaning of the sentence.

> The woman who just entered is my sister. (Restrictive. *Who just entered* identifies which woman.)
>
> My sister, who is wearing a red coat, is an accountant. (Nonrestrictive. *Who is wearing a red coat* describes but does not change the meaning of the subject *sister.*)
>
> This magazine, *Newsweek,* is very informative. (Nonrestrictive. *Newsweek* describes the subject, *magazine,* by giving its name but does not change the meaning of the sentence.)
>
> The magazine *Newsweek* is very informative. (Restrictive. Here the name of the magazine is vital to the meaning of the sentence. The speaker or writer limits or *restricts,* the quality of being *very informative* to this one magazine in a sentence that indicates a consideration of many or all magazines.)

PARENTHETICAL EXPRESSIONS

Use commas to set off a word, phrase, or clause that interrupts the natural flow of the sentence.

accordingly	for example
as a consequence	however
as a result	I believe
as a rule	if any
as well as...	if necessary
as you know	in addition
by the way	in brief

in fact	of course
it has been said	on the contrary
it seems	on the other hand
I understand	therefore
moreover	to be sure
nevertheless	together with...

We have, I believe, two days left.
Mr. Smith, as well as his assistant, will be leaving early.
We will, nevertheless, proceed as scheduled.

If any of the expressions above are used in a manner that will not interrupt the natural flow of the sentence, do not use commas.

However experienced he may be, he will not qualify for the position. (*However* is part of the introductory phrase.)

QUOTATIONS

Use commas to identify a person who is being directly quoted.

"I will not arrive until much later," he said.
He said, "I will not arrive until much later."

The comma and period at the end of quoted material always go *inside* the quotation mark.

SERIES

Use commas to separate a series of three or more items unless a conjunction is placed between each.

He enjoys reading and swimming. (two items)
He enjoys reading, swimming, and bowling. (three
   items)
He enjoys reading and swimming and bowling. (conjunctions)

In a sentence like the second example above, a comma should be placed before the final conjunction to avoid misreading. Do not use a comma before the final *and* or ampersand symbol (&) within the name of a company.

He is a member of Gold, Smith & Weston.

TITLES, DEGREES, AND ABBREVIATIONS

Use commas to set off abbreviations, titles, and degrees that follow a name. Always use commas before *Inc.* and *Ltd.*

Thomas James, Jr., is our newly elected chairman.
Max Lorenz, C.P.A., will be our guest speaker.
ABC Realty Co., Inc., is moving to the South.
Walter McNicholas, Esq., is a promising attorney.

If you use *Esq.* after the name of an attorney or *M.D.* after the name of a doctor, drop the prefixes *Mr.*, *Dr.*, etc.
   Roman numerals following a person's name are not set off with commas.

Thomas James II is our newly elected chairman.

VERBALS

Use a comma following an introductory verbal phrase (a phrase beginning with an infinitive or with a verb ending *ed* or *ing*) when it is used to modify the remainder of the sentence.

To prove his point, he checked the reference book.
Provoked, he slammed the door behind him.
Lacking confidence, the boy did not enter the contest.

MISCELLANEOUS

1. Use commas to set off adjectives that follow the noun they are modifying.

   The cashier, frustrated and exhausted, located the error.

2. Use commas to set off contrasting expressions such as *not, never, seldom.*

   I saw him in March, not April.
   He always teaches sociology, never psychology.

3. Use a comma to divide a sentence that starts as a statement and ends as a question.

   You will call him, won't you? (This type of sentence will always end with a question mark.)

4. Use commas to separate items in reference works.

   You will find that information in Volume III, Chapter 2, page 12, line 2.

5. Use commas to separate words that are repeated for emphasis.

   He told me that story many, many times.

6. Use commas to clarify numerals that have four or more digits.

   $1,000   4,356 votes   12,000 words

Exceptions include telephone numbers, years, serial numbers, ZIP codes, invoice numbers, policy numbers, and the like.

   352-8198   Policy No. 110285641   10952 (ZIP)

7. Use commas in sentences that would be confusing if they were omitted.

   Only one week before, I had lunch with him. (Without the comma, you would have a sentence fragment.)

8. Use commas to indicate that readily understood words have been omitted.

   Theodore will be given $500; Susan, $300; and Bob, $200. (After *Susan* and after *Bob* the words *will be given* have been omitted.)

9. Use a comma after the complimentary closing of a letter, except when you are using open punctuation. (See the "Standard Letter Parts" section of chapter 10 for more information about open punctuation.)

   Sincerely yours,   Respectfully yours,
   Very truly yours,   Cordially yours,

   Note that only the first word of the complimentary closing is capitalized.

10. Use a comma to separate two sets of figures that are not related.

    Since 1958, 500 machines have been sold.

11. Use a comma after inverted names such as on a list or in a file.

    Coleman, Russell (*Russell* is the first name.)

12. Use a comma to separate a phrase from the rest of the sentence when the phrase is inverted or taken out of its natural order.

    For me, it will mean more work and less pay.

13. Use a comma to separate two adjectives in a series, provided the word *and* could be used between the two.

    She is an intelligent, thoughtful person. (The word *and* could be placed between: *intelligent and thoughtful.*)
    These three old manual typewriters are in need of repair. (The word *and* could not logically be placed between *three old manual.*)

Semicolons

The semicolon (;) has often been referred to as a weak period or a strong comma. It is a useful mark of punctuation, but it should be used sparingly.

1. Use a semicolon to separate independent clauses in a compound sentence when no conjunction is used to join the clauses.

You need not send any money now; we will bill you later. (Two independent clauses: *You need not send any money now. We will bill you later.*)

You need not send any money, for we will bill you later. (When a conjunction is used, a comma will separate the clauses.)

2. Use a semicolon to separate independent clauses joined by a conjunction (such as *and, but, or, nor*) if two or more commas are used in either clause and if the semicolon will prevent misreading.

I thought I had met everyone in your family; but James, the youngest, told me that you have a sister who lives in Canada.

I like red, blue, and green; but she likes brown, black, and rust.

3. Use a semicolon between coordinate clauses of a compound sentence when they are joined by transitional (parenthetical) words and phrases. (Check the list of parenthetical expressions given in the "Commas" section of this chapter.)

The jury has been deliberating for two days; however, they have not reached a decision.

President Smith has approved a new tax cut; therefore, we should start to see more money in our paychecks.

4. Use a semicolon to separate items in a series when the items themselves contain commas.

He was available on Monday, January 5; Tuesday, January 6; and Wednesday, January 7.

I will be giving special awards to Alma Kuhn, sec-retary; Warren Bergstein, accountant; and Fran Haber, teacher.

5. Use a semicolon before expressions such as *for example, that is, for instance, that is to say,* or *namely.*

The paint is available in three colors; namely, red, blue, and beige.

Many of our policies will change this year; for example, our salespeople will be paid on a commission basis.

Colons

The colon (:) indicates the strongest possible break in a sentence and often draws the reader's attention to that which follows.

1. Use a colon after a formal introduction that includes (or implies) the phrase *the following.*

You should know how to use the following office machines: a typewriter, a duplicator, and a calculator.

We expect to open branch offices in each of these states: California, Nevada, and Oregon. (*The following* is implied.)

You should not use a colon after the main verb in a sentence.

Her most difficult subjects are English, science, and mathematics. (*Are* is the main verb.)

2. Use a colon to introduce a long direct quotation.

    Congressman Gilroy said: "I know the importance of winning, but it is not worth your while to get yourself involved in that scheme."

3. Use a colon after a statement that introduces an explanation or an example.

    My final recommendation is this: Do not delay.

4. Use a colon after the salutation of a business letter unless you are using open punctuation (see chapter 10, "Standard Letter Parts").

    Gentlemen: Dear Mr. Jones:
    Dear Sir: My dear Miss Smith:

5. Use a colon to separate hours and minutes when expressed in figures. Omit the :00 when expressing time as an even clock hour.

    4:30 p.m.   2:45 a.m.
    3 p.m.   5 a.m.

    NOTE: Refer to the "Numbers" chapter for further rules regarding clock hours.

Dashes

The dash (—) is a very emphatic mark of punctuation used for emphasis or visual effect. Use it sparingly, because the overuse of it diminishes its effect. When typing the dash, use two hyphens,* and do not leave a space before, after, or in between.

1. Use dashes to set off a parenthetical expression or an appositive that you want to emphasize.

   Have you attended a convention in New Jersey's most famous resort—Altantic City? (instead of comma)
   The book—in case you are interested—is very informative.

2. Use a dash before a word (such as *these, any, all, each*) that sums up a preceding series.

   Pies, cheesecakes, and tarts—these are our specialties.
   Lynne Sullivan, Janice Teisch, and Ann Kraft—these are my friends from school.

3. Use a dash to indicate a summarizing thought or an afterthought added to the end of a sentence.

   That course was a big help to me—I liked it.
   I am sure that was not an easy decision—not even for you. (more emphasis than a comma)

4. Use a dash before the name of an author or work that follows a direct quotation and gives its source.

   "Ask not what your country can do for you. Ask what you can do for your country."—John F. Kennedy

---

*A separate treatment of hyphens has not been included in this chapter. For information about the uses of this punctuation mark, see chapter 2, "Compound Adjectives"; chapter 4, "Hyphenated Numbers"; and chapter 5, under the "Do's" of word division.

"English is undoubtedly the most important of the
world's languages at the present time."—*Webster's
New Collegiate Dictionary*

5. Use dashes to emphasize an independent clause that has
abruptly interrupted the main thought of a sentence.

I was certain that our manager—he more than anyone
else I know—would have recommended Jim for
that promotion.

Parentheses

Parentheses ( ) are used in somewhat the same fashion as
dashes, only they tend to de-emphasize the conveyed message.
The degree of emphasis to be conveyed is the choice of the
writer.

1. Use parentheses to set off parenthetical expressions or
appositives that you want to de-emphasize.

She returned to New York (her favorite city) for her
vacation.

2. Use parentheses to set off references to charts, pages,
diagrams, illustrations, chapters of books, etc.

The section on philosophy (pages 200–260) should
be very helpful to you.

3. Parentheses may be used to enclose numerals or letters
that precede items in a series that are in sentence form.

The countries to be visited are (1) England, (2) France,
(3) Italy, and (4) Spain.

For lists in columns, any of the following forms may be used:

1)	1.	(1)
2)	2.	(2)
3)	3.	(3)

4. Use parentheses in formal writing, such as legal documents, when the writer wants to use both the spelled-out number and the written number.

> The Purchaser agrees to pay to the Seller the sum of ONE THOUSAND and 00/100 DOLLARS ($1,000.00).

5. If the item in parentheses falls inside the sentence, the sentence punctuation should be placed outside the parentheses.

> Stationery often measures 8½ by 11 inches (216 by 279 millimeters).
> When you call (hopefully today), I should have the answer.

6. If the item in parentheses is a complete sentence, the mark of punctuation will go inside the parentheses.

> Dr. Harold Siegelbaum is a gynecologist. (Dr. Louis Lefkowitz is a gynecologist and obstetrician.)

Brackets

Brackets ([ ]) are not always a standard key on the typewriter and may have to be inserted by hand.

1. In quoted material, use brackets to enclose anything added by someone other than the writer or speaker.

   He said, "The length of the trial [from June 15 to September 16] caused great inconvenience to the jurors."

2. Use brackets to enclose parenthetical information within a larger parenthesis.

   Your order (which included a ream of paper and a dozen pencils [markers are unavailable]) was delivered on Monday.

   Keep in mind that brackets are rarely used in business writing. They are generally found in printed material.

Underscores

1. Use an underscore (_____) to set off the titles of books, magazines, newspapers, pamphlets, brochures, long poems, movies, plays, and other literary works.

   I read The New York Times every day.

   An alternative is to completely capitalize the title.

   I read THE NEW YORK TIMES every day.

2. Use underscores with foreign expressions that may be unfamiliar to the reader.

   The attorney introduced prima facie evidence.

Quotation Marks

Quotation marks (" ") are extremely important marks of punctuation and must be used properly.

1. Use quotation marks to enclose material that is directly quoted; that is, the exact words of what was originally said or written.

   "I saw your advertisement in the newspaper," he said.

   Do not put quotation marks around an indirect quotation; that is, a rewording of the original statement.

   He said that he had seen your advertisement in the newspaper.

2. Use quotation marks to enclose titles of articles, short poems, lectures or topics, paintings, short stories, or chapter names of books. Check the chapter on "Capitalization" for further rules.

   In *Webster's Legal Secretaries Handbook* there is a very informative chapter entitled "Preparing and Typewriting Client Documents."

3. Unless otherwise punctuated, use quotation marks to set off words or phrases introduced by any of the following expressions: *the word, the term, known as, marked, termed, called, entitled.*

   The check was marked "cancelled."

4. Use quotation marks around familiar words used in an unusual or unconventional manner.

   My brother thinks he is "hot stuff."

5. Use single quotation marks to set off a quotation that appears within a quotation.

   The student asked, "How do I spell the word 'accommodate'?"

6. When quoting lengthy material, you should place the quotation mark at the beginning of each paragraph and at the end of the final paragraph only.

   " ⸺⸺⸺⸺⸺⸺⸺⸺⸺⸺⸺⸺⸺⸺⸺⸺⸺⸺⸺
   ⸺⸺⸺⸺⸺⸺⸺⸺⸺⸺⸺⸺⸺⸺⸺⸺⸺⸺⸺⸺
   ⸺⸺⸺⸺⸺⸺⸺⸺⸺⸺⸺⸺⸺⸺⸺⸺⸺⸺⸺.

   " ⸺⸺⸺⸺⸺⸺⸺⸺⸺⸺⸺⸺⸺⸺⸺⸺⸺⸺⸺
   ⸺⸺⸺⸺⸺⸺⸺⸺⸺⸺⸺⸺⸺⸺⸺⸺⸺⸺⸺⸺
   ⸺⸺⸺⸺⸺⸺⸺⸺⸺⸺⸺⸺⸺⸺⸺⸺ ."

QUOTATION MARKS AND OTHER PUNCTUATION

1. Always place the period and comma *inside* the quotes.

   He commented, "They already left."
   "They already left," he commented.

2. Always place the semicolon and colon *outside* the quotes.

   He said, "I will see you about noon"; however, it is already one.

3. A question mark and exclamation point will go inside the quoted material when it applies to the quoted material *only*. It will go outside when it applies to the entire sentence.

She asked, "Did you enjoy your trip?" (The quoted material alone is the question, not the entire sentence.)

Why did you call me "impossible"? (The entire sentence is a question.)

Ellipses

Use an ellipsis (...) to indicate what words are being omitted from the original quoted material. Space once before, between, and after each period. If indicating the omission of the end of a sentence, a complete sentence, or more, use four periods (....).

"Let everyone mind his own business, and endeavor to be what he was made. ... If a man does not keep pace with his companions, perhaps it is because he hears a different drummer. Let him step to the music which he hears, however measured or far away."—Thoreau

Periods

The period (.) is probably the most common punctuation mark.

1. Use the period at the conclusion of a statement, a request (even when phrased politely as a question), or command.

I very much appreciate your consideration.

May I hear from you at your earliest convenience. (a polite request)

2. Use the period in writing some abbreviations. (Many abbreviations are now being used without the period.)

Dr.	Mrs.	Ph.D.
Inc.	Co.	a.m.
FBI	YMCA	NAACP
NATO	TVA	CIA

When a sentence ends with an abbreviation, one period is used which represents both the abbreviation and the end of the sentence.

I purchased my sofa from A & D Interiors, Inc.

3. The period is used as a decimal point.

Our profits have increased by 13.5 percent.

4. Use the period to separate dollars from cents.

I purchased the blouse for $28.50.

Question Marks

1. Use a question mark to conclude a direct question.

When may we expect you?

2. Use a question mark after each question in a series of short questions that relate to the same subject and verb.

Can you join us on March 16? March 17? March 18?

3. Use a question mark when a sentence begins as a statement and ends as a question.

> You made the delivery, didn't you?

4. Use a question mark in parentheses to indicate uncertainty about a stated fact.

> You ordered ten (?) copies of the book.

5. If a question ends with an abbreviation, place the question mark after the period.

> Did you purchase that at ABC Stores, Inc.?

Exclamation Points

The exclamation point (!) is used after a word or group of words that express strong feelings (such as anger, relief, fear, excitement, surprise).

> That is an absolutely incredible story!
> "Look out!" the man shouted.

Apostrophes

The apostrophe (') is used primarily to indicate an omission or to show possession.

1. Use an apostrophe to indicate that there has been an omission in a number or a word.

> '89 (1989)
> didn't (did not)
> I've (I have)

In formal writing, however, it is proper to avoid contractions, when possible.

Formal: I will call as soon as I have returned.
Informal: I'll call as soon as I've returned.

2. Form the possessive of a singular noun by adding an apostrophe and an *s*.

the cat's meow	the baby's bottle
Sue's coat	Mr. Jones's car
your boss's desk	the lady's umbrella

3. Form the possessive of a plural noun that ends in *s* by adding an apostrophe only.

two cats' food	the babies' bottles
the girls' coats	the Joneses' car
your bosses' desks	the ladies' umbrellas

4. Form the possessive of an irregular plural noun (one that does not end in *s*) by adding an apostrophe and an *s*.

your teeth's condition	children's toys
women's hats	oxen's hoofs
salespeople's commissions	foremen's influence

5. Use the apostrophe in common expressions referring to time, distance, value, or measurement.

yesterday's news	a moment's notice
a month's vacation	three months' vacation
five miles' distance	a year's salary

6. Use the apostrophe after the period in order to make an abbreviation possessive.

The M.B.A.'s thesis
ABC Realty Co.'s contracts
the M.D.'s opinion

7. Use the apostrophe to indicate possession at the end of a compound word.

> sister-in-law's car
> sisters-in-law's cars
> the secretary-treasurer's report
> everybody's responsibility

8. Use the apostrophe to indicate the plural form of numbers, letters, and symbols.

> He has three *i*'s in his name.
> He gave me three 20's as
> change.

9. Use the apostrophe after the last of two or more nouns in order to indicate joint ownership.

> Judy and Joan's locker
> Joe and Al's car

10. Use the apostrophe after each noun in order to indicate individual ownership.

> Judy's and Joan's lockers
> Joe's and Al's cars

11. The apostrophe is generally omitted in names of organizations, magazines, etc.

> State Teachers College
> Bankers Trust Company

Asterisks

The asterisk (*) is used infrequently.

1. Use the asterisk to refer the reader to a footnote at the bottom of the page.

   "It's been noted of Vermont winters that when one isn't currently in progress, one either will be shortly or was recently."*

2. Use the asterisk to indicate the omission of words that are unfit for printing or the omission of an entire paragraph.

   How dare you call him a •••!

   It is of no consequence to Sir Thomas whether or not her visit proves enjoyable so long as she learns to respect the wealth that she has lived in at Mansfield.

   *   *   *

   Jane's stay at Portsmouth does, in fact, make her long for her childhood home, though not for the reasons Sir Thomas had intended.

Diagonals or Slashes

1. Use the diagonal or slash (/) in certain abbreviations and expressions of time.

---

*Brian Vachon, "Winter in Vermont," *Vista*, Winter 1981–82, p. 4.

c/o (care of)   3/4 (fraction)
B/L (bill of lading)   1987/88

2. Use the diagonal for *and/or* expressions.

Sales/advertising will be located in this office.

CHAPTER 2

GRAMMAR

Adjectives, Adverbs, Conjunctions, Nouns, Prepositions, Pronouns, Verbs, Super Stumpers, Subject and Verb Agreement

Grammar, as defined in *Webster's New Collegiate Dictionary*, is "the study of the classes of words, their inflections, and their functions and relations in the sentence..." This chapter presents in alphabetical order the major parts of speech with explanations and examples of correct usage.

Adjectives

An adjective is a word, a phrase, or a clause that either modifies, describes, or limits the noun or pronoun it is describing. When used properly, the adjective can transform an ordinary sentence into a very colorful one.

> The darkly charred steak sizzled on the grill—its top beaded with hot, red juices.
> *as opposed to*
> The steak cooked on the grill.

An adjective will answer the questions: What kind? Which? What color? How many? What size?

28

red dress   *rainy* day
this book   *five* dozen
good friend   *less* expensive
linen curtains   *difficult* task
several ideas

Adjectives take different forms according to the noun or nouns they modify. The positive degree is the form of the adjective used when no comparison is being made. The comparative degree is the form of the adjective that compares two things or people. The superlative degree compares three or more things or people.

Positive	Comparative	Superlative
big	bigger	biggest
cold	colder	coldest
pretty	prettier	prettiest
young	younger	youngest
heavy	heavier	heaviest
fine	finer	finest

When the positive adjective is one syllable, an *er* forms the comparative degree and an *est* forms the superlative degree. This rule also holds true for some two syllable words. For many words ending in *y*, you must change the *y* to *i* and add *er* or *est*. When the positive adjective is two syllables or more, you most often use *more* or *less* with the comparative degree and *most* or *least* with the superlative degree. *More* and *most* indicate increasing amounts and *less* and *least* indicate decreasing amounts.

Positive	Comparative	Superlative
active	more active	most active
	less active	least active

successful	more successful	most successful
	less successful	least successful
careful	more careful	most careful
	less careful	least careful
capable	more capable	most capable
	less capable	least capable
fortunate	more fortunate	most fortunate
	less fortunate	least fortunate

That is a *big* building.
That building is the *bigger* of the two.
That building is the *biggest* of all.
He is a *successful* actor.
He is a *more successful* actor than his brother.
He is the *most successful* actor in our group.

A few adjectives have irregular comparative and superlative degrees.

Positive	**Comparative**	**Superlative**
good or well	better	best
far (distance)	farther	farthest
far (degree)	further	furthest
much or many	more	most
little (amount)	less	least
little (size)	littler	littlest
bad or ill	worse	worst

Some adjectives, because of their meaning, are absolute and cannot be compared.

dead	genuine
exact	always
square	perfect
impossible	round
unique	wrong

never   correct
empty   accurate
stationary

NOTE: If something is *exact*, for example, that is an absolute degree. A thing cannot be more or less exact.

COMPOUND ADJECTIVES

In many cases it is necessary to join two adjectives together (using a hyphen) so that they form a single description.

I have twenty-one dollar bills. ($21)
I have twenty one-dollar bills. ($20)
a light-blue coat
a part-time job
bumper-to-bumper traffic

To require a hyphen, the adjective must come before the noun it is modifying.

That is a well-written report.
That report is well written.

Use more than one hyphen when an idea has one noun ending but two or more adjectives to describe it.

a two- or three-year lease
a part- or full-time job
a 50-, 60-, or 70-person capacity

Note the spacing and the use of commas above.
Exceptions to this rule are as follows:
1. Do not use a hyphen between adjectives if the first adjective ends in *est* or *ly*. (a newly completed house, the freshest cut flowers)

2. Do not use a hyphen between a number and the word *percent*. (a ten percent discount)
3. Do not use a hyphen with expressions that you automatically think of as one, such as *social security tax, real estate office, word processing system, life insurance policy*. *Coordinate Adjectives:* When two or more adjectives are not joined by *and, or,* or *nor* and they are modifying the same noun, a comma will take the place of the conjunctions.

an efficient, reliable secretary
an efficient and reliable secretary
a sincere, intelligent face
a sincere and intelligent face
a long, winding road
a long and winding road

If the word *and* does not sound right between the adjectives, omit the comma.

I purchased a new green car. (Although *new* and *green* are adjectives, you would not say *a new and green car.*)
Her bright red dress complemented her shiny black hair.

ARTICLES

The adjectives *a* and *an* are also called indefinite articles. They are indefinite because they do not refer to a specific object; for example, *the book* is specific whereas *a book* is not.

The use of *a* or *an* is determined by the *sound* of the word that immediately follows. If the word begins with a consonant sound, use the article *a*. If the word begins with a vowel sound, use the article *an*.

a device   a unique design
a mile   an onion
a two-week trip   an heir (vowel sound)
a home   an X-ray (vowel sound)
a high level   an error
a call   an illness

Adverbs

An adverb is a word that modifies a verb, an adjective, or another adverb. It answers the questions: How? When? Why? How much? Where? To what degree?

Adverbs take different forms for the positive, comparative, and superlative degrees. The positive degree is the form of the adverb used when no comparison is being made. The comparative degree is the form of the adverb used for comparing two things. The superlative degree compares three or more things.

Positive	Comparative	Superlative
fast	faster	fastest
effectively	more effectively	most effectively
	less effectively	least effectively

Many adjectives function as adverbs as well. Many remain the same in both forms; others require the addition of *ly*.

His handwriting is *legible*. (adjective)
He writes *legibly*. (adverb)
The senator's speech was *brief*. (adjective)
The senator spoke *briefly*. (adverb)

Adverbs are used to describe the senses (see, taste, feel, smell, and hear). Adjectives are used to describe these verbs when the modifier refers to the condition of the subject.

> The red rose smells *sweet.* (adjective referring to condition)
> The *sweetly* scented perfume had a very strong odor. (adverb describing the adjective *scented*)

DOUBLE NEGATIVES

Never use two negative words to express a single negative idea.

> Right: We *do not* require *any* more information.
> Wrong: We *do not* require *no* more information.
> Right: I can *hardly* believe my eyes.
> Wrong: I *can't hardly* believe my eyes.

Remember that *hardly* and *scarcely* express a negative idea— no other negative word is necessary in sentences in which either one appears.

Two of the most commonly confused adjectives and adverbs are *real* and *really* and *good* and *well.*

real (adjective meaning *genuine*)
really (adverb meaning *actually*)

> Are you wearing *real* cowboy boots?
> I had a *really* good time at the party.

good (adjective meaning *praiseworthy*)
well (adverb referring to health)

> You did a *good* job repairing the chair.
> I do not feel *well* today.

Conjunctions

A conjunction is a word that connects two words, phrases, or clauses. Three types are coordinate, correlative, and subordinate.

COORDINATE CONJUNCTIONS

These are used to join two or more words, phrases, or clauses that are equal in construction and grammatical rank.

and	but
or	nor
for	yet
so	whereas (legal term)

I read the book, *and* I enjoyed it very much.
I read the book *and* enjoyed it very much.

NOTE: For comma rules accompanying conjunctions, refer to the "Punctuation" chapter.

CORRELATIVE CONJUNCTIONS

These are used in pairs and join the elements of a sentence.

both/and	either/or
so/as	neither/nor
not only/but also	as/as
whether/or	whether/or not

I have read *neither* his report *nor* his letters.
Both Paula *and* her sister are out at a movie.

SUBORDINATE CONJUNCTIONS

These connect a subordinate (dependent) clause to the main clause. The clauses they introduce always function as adverbs, adjectives, or nouns within a complete sentence. The following are commonly used subordinate conjunctions:

after	provided that
although	since
as	so . . . as
as . . . as	so that
as if	than
as long as	that
as soon as	though
as though	till
because	unless
before	until
even if	when
even though	whenever
except	where
if	wherever
in order that	whether
provided	while

Please tell me *when* the group arrives. (*When* serves as a subordinate conjunction and does not have a comma placed before it.)

When the group arrives, please tell me. (An adverb clause introduced with a subordinate conjunction does require a comma.)

Nouns

A noun is a person, a place, or a thing and can be either proper or common. A proper noun should be capitalized and a common noun should not.

Proper Nouns	Common Nouns
New York City	city
Royale Theater	theater
Spring Valley High School	high school
Main Street	street

A **collective noun** identifies a group, company, council, audience, faculty, union, team, jury, committee, etc. When the group is acting as a unit, use a singular verb; when the group is acting as independent members, use a plural verb.

The *family is* going to Cancún for vacation.
The *family are* going on separate vacations this year.
The *jury is* deliberating.
The *jury are* going home.

NOTE: Refer to the "Spelling" chapter for the formation of plural nouns.

Prepositions

A preposition is a connecting word that shows the relationship between words in a sentence.

above	below	in
about	beneath	inside
across	beside	into
after	between	like
against	beyond	near
along	by	of
among	down	off
around	during	on
at	except	since
before	for	to
behind	from	toward

through	up	within
under	upon	
until	with	

Listed below are some commonly confused prepositions:

accompany by (a person)
accompany with (an object)

> Mrs. Jones was *accompanied by* her son.
> The carriage was *accompanied with* assembling instructions.

account for (something or someone)
account to (someone)

> I cannot *account for* his behavior.
> The cashier had to *account to* the manager for the shortage.

agree to (someone else's plan)
agree with (have same opinion)

> I will *agree to* the terms of our contract.
> I *agree with* you about the terms of our contract.

angry at or about (something)
angry with (someone)

> He was *angry about* the outcome of the discussion.
> I hope you will not be *angry with* me.

apply for (a position)
apply to (someone or something)

> I am going to *apply for* the job in the newspaper.
> I am going to *apply to* that company for a job.

argue about (something)
argue with (someone)

> I do not want to *argue about* the problem.
> I do not want to *argue with* you about the problem.

compare to (show similarity)
compare with (examine for similarities and differences)

> You can *compare* that restaurant *to* the best.
> She *compared* my acting *with* Marilyn Monroe's.

compensate for

> The attorney was *compensated for* his time.

comply with

> Will you *comply with* the orders?

consists in (exists in)
consists of (comprised of)

> Happiness *consists in* knowing you are loved.
> The books *consists of* 15 chapters.

convenient for (suitable)
convenient to (close)

> Will Monday morning be *convenient for* you?
> The new shopping center should be *convenient to* all
> forms of transportation.

correspond to (agree with)
correspond with (write letters)

> The merchandise does not *correspond to* your ad.
> I *correspond with* my pen pal regularly.

depend on (rely)

> You can *depend on* me to get the job done.

differ about (something)
differ from (to be unlike)
differ with (someone)

> We *differ about* ways to perform the task.
> I *differ from* you in many ways.
> I *differ with* you over the projected outcome.

different from (never *than*)

> This new typewriter is *different from* the one I had.

encroach on (infringe on)

> The pool *encroaches on* your neighbor's property.

indicative of

> This attempt is *indicative of* my capabilities.

liable for (responsible)
liable to (susceptible)

> You will be *liable for* any damage to my car.
> You are *liable to* have a heart attack if you do not
> slow down.

parallel to

> Main Street is *parallel to* Lafayette Avenue.

rely on (or *upon*)

> You can *rely on* me to finish what I start.

reminiscent of

> The movie was *reminiscent of* the "good old days."

responsible for

> You are *responsible for* your own actions.

retroactive to (not *from*)

> Your increase will be *retroactive to* January 1.

speak to (tell something to)
speak with (discuss with)

> I will *speak to* the students about this situation.
> If you *speak with* me, we can find a solution.

specialize in

> She will *specialize in* computers and data processing.

talk to (address)
talk with (discuss)

> The visitor *talked to* the audience for an hour.
> I *talked with* my teacher about the problem.

Pronouns

A pronoun is a word used in place of a noun or a name. Its main purpose is to eliminate the need for awkward and monotonous repetition.

The noun that the pronoun replaces is called its *antecedent*. The pronoun must agree with its antecedent in person, number, and gender.

When *Mr. Jones* arrives, please have *him* fill out an application.

When *Mrs. Jones* arrives, please have *her* fill out an application.

When the *applicants* arrive, *they* should first fill out applications.

If you have difficulty mastering the use of pronouns, the chart on the following page should be of value.

The **nominative** case is used (1) when the pronoun is the subject of the sentence, or (2) when it follows any form of the verb *to be* (*be, am, is, are, was, were, been, being, will be, has been,* etc.).

I will call her in the morning. (*I* is the subject.)

We will complete the project tomorrow. (*We* is the subject.)

Is Barbara there? Yes, this is *she*. (*She* follows *is*.)

It was *we* who sponsored the carnival. (*We* follows *was*.)

The **objective** case is used (1) when the pronoun is the object of the verb, or (2) when it is the object of a preposition. An object always answers the question: Whom? What?

They all congratulated *her*. (congratulated whom?)

The doctor gave *him* a prescription. (gave whom?)

Please give *it* to Stan and *me*. (what? to whom?)

Mr. Peterson talked with *them* about the assignment. (with whom?)

The **possessive** case is used to indicate possession, kind, origin, brand, authorship, etc.

The decision is completely *yours*.

That new car has lost *its* shine. (not *it's*)

CASE:	NOMINATIVE		OBJECTIVE		POSSESSIVE	
Number:	Singular	Plural	Singular	Plural	Singular	Plural
First Person	I	we	me	us	my mine	our ours
Second Person	you	you	you	you	your yours	your yours
Third Person (masculine)	he	they	him	them	his	their theirs
Third Person (feminine)	she	they	her	them	her hers	their theirs
Neuter	it	they	it	them	its	their theirs

When using the possessive case, do not add apostrophe *s* (*'s*) because the pronoun itself is already possessive.

> That is *our* book.
> That book is *ours*. (not *our's*)

If you have difficulty with these rules, either complete the sentence mentally or use each pronoun individually. The correct pronoun will then usually be obvious.

> Eric can play the violin better than *I*. (I can)
> They have called as often as *we*. (we have called)
> The attendant stopped Marc and *me* at the gate.
>   (stopped Marc at the gate, stopped me at the gate)
> Do you want *her* or *me*? (Do you want her? Do you want me?)
> *We* secretaries have a very responsible job. (We have)
> Is Bob older or younger than *he*? (than he is)

NOTE: When speaking of another person and yourself, always mention yourself last.

Be certain that your pronoun refers clearly to a definite person, place, or thing. To do so, ask yourself to whom or what the pronoun refers.

> The salesman told Mr. Kraft that *he* does not understand the problem. (*Unclear*: who does not understand the problem? The salesman? Mr. Kraft?)
> Dick Lehnert said that he would like to return to the United States. (*Clear*: "he" clearly refers to Dick Lehnert.)

The following pronouns are always singular and take a singular verb and pronouns.

anybody	anything
anyone	each

either	nobody
everybody	nothing
everyone	one
everything	somebody
much	someone
neither	something

Each of these people *is* to be notified.
Everyone has his or *her* own problems.
Neither of Gary's proposals *is* acceptable.

Some one, any one, every one will always be written as two words when the word *of* follows.

Any one of these people will be satisfactory.
If *anyone* calls, I will be in Mr. Barton's office.

The following pronouns are always plural and take a plural verb or pronoun.

both	few	others
many	several	

Both of the congressmen will air *their* views.
Few of the stores *are* closed for the holiday.

The following pronouns may be either singular or plural depending on the antecedent.

all	more	none
any	most	some

All of the *fruit is* finished. (*Fruit* is used as a singular noun.)
None of the *money is* available. (*Money* is used as a singular noun.)
None of the *men are* available. (*Men* is a plural noun.)

WHO AND WHOM

No longer is there any need for confusion! Always use the pronoun *who* when you can substitute the words *he, she,* or *they* for it.

> This company needs a person *who* knows chemistry. (She knows chemistry.)
> We always remember people *who* are thoughtful. (He is thoughtful.)
> There are many people *who* will not understand. (They will not understand.)

Always use the pronoun *whom* when you can substitute the words *him, her,* or *them* for it.

> To *Whom* This May Concern: (This may concern her.)
> Are you the gentleman to *whom* I spoke yesterday? (I spoke to him yesterday.)
> Mark Twain is a writer *whom* we will never forget. (We will never forget him.)

The same rule applies to *whoever* and *whomever.*

> Please give me the identity of *whoever* made the donation. (He made the donation.)
> I will be delighted to contact *whomever* you recommend. (You recommend them.)

Who and *whom* refer only to people. *That* refers to people, places, and things when introducing essential clauses.

> I need the name of a car dealer *that* has a Citation available.

Which refers to people, places, and things when introducing nonessential clauses.

> The policy *which* we adopted is the best for our situation.

Verbs

The verb is the most important part of the sentence because it expresses an action, a condition, or a state of being. It makes a statement about the subject.

> Mr. Jones *strolls* through the store.
> Mr. Jones *rushed* through the store.
> Mr. Jones *will stroll* through the store.
> Mr. Jones *is rushing* through the store.

The verb tells you whether the action is present, past, in the future, or in progress. The verb tenses are as follows:

present action now happening or in progress
past action was started or has been completed
future action has not yet taken place
present perfect action has been completed, will continue, or may occur again
past perfect action was completed prior to another past action or past time
future perfect action will be completed before a specified time

> I *walk* to school. (present)
> I *walked* to school. (past)
> I *shall walk* to school. (future)
> I *have walked* to school. (present perfect)
> I *had walked* to school. (past perfect)

By tomorrow, I *shall have walked* to school. (future
  perfect)

When verbs are expressed in the present or past tenses,
they are likely to be single words. The remaining tenses, however, require the aid of helping verbs.

The chart on pages 56–57 indicates verb conjugation, with
the tenses; first, second, and third persons singular and plural;
and the helping verbs.

Not all verbs are regular; that is, they do not have *ed* added
to the past and perfect tenses. In irregular verbs either the
root of the word changes to indicate past and perfect or it
remains the same and no ending is added.

The following list gives proper forms for many irregular
verbs.

Present	Past	Perfect
be, am, is, are	was	been
bear	bore	borne
beat	beat	beaten
begin	began	begun
bid (offer price)	bid	bid
bite	bit	bitten
blow	blew	blown
break	broke	broken
bring	brought	brought
build	built	built
burst	burst	burst
buy	bought	bought
catch	caught	caught
choose	chose	chosen
cling	clung	clung
come	came	come
cost	cost	cost

creep	crept	crept
deal	dealt	dealt
dig	dug	dug
drink	drank	drunk
drive	drove	driven
do	did	done
draw	drew	drawn
eat	ate	eaten
fall	fell	fallen
fight	fought	fought
find	found	found
fly	flew	flown
forecast	forecast(ed)	forecast(ed)
forget	forgot	forgotten
freeze	froze	frozen
get	got	got, gotten
give	gave	given
go	went	gone
grind	ground	ground
grow	grew	grown
hang (an object)	hung	hung
hang (a person)	hanged	hanged
have, has	had	had
hit	hit	hit
hurt	hurt	hurt
know	knew	known
lead	led	led
lay (place)	laid	laid
lie (recline)	lay	lain
lie (falsehood)	lied	lied
make	made	made
meet	met	met
pay	paid	paid
prove	proved	proved, proven
put	put	put

quit	quit	quit
raise (lift)	raised	raised
ride	rode	ridden
ring (bell)	rang	rung
rise	rose	risen
run	ran	run
see	saw	seen
seek	sought	sought
sell	sold	sold
set	set	set
shake	shook	shaken
shine (give light)	shone	shone
shine (polish)	shined	shined
show	showed	shown, showed
shrink	shrank	shrunk
sing	sang	sung
sink	sank	sunk
sit (rest)	sat	sat
speak	spoke	spoken
spend	spent	spent
spring	sprang	sprung
steal	stole	stolen
sting	stung	stung
strike	struck	struck, stricken
swear	swore	sworn
swim	swam	swum
swing	swung	swung
take	took	taken
teach	taught	taught
tear	tore	torn
tell	told	told
think	thought	thought
throw	threw	thrown
wear	wore	worn
win	won	won

| wring | wrung | wrung |
| write | wrote | written |

SPECIAL VERB PROBLEMS

1. Two sets of helping verbs that seem to cause difficulty are *can* and *may* and *could* and *might*.

    Can denotes the ability or capacity to do something in the present or future while *could* denotes either the ability or capacity to do something in the past or a future possibility.

   She *can* see you now. (present)
   I *can* arrive early tomorrow. (future)
   Yesterday he *could* not be reached. (past)
   The report *could* be completed in three days. (future)

    May denotes a request for permission or a possibility in the present tense while *might* denotes a request for permission or a possibility in the past or future tenses.

   May we leave early? (Polite request)
   There *might* be a reasonable explanation for their ac-
   tions.
   We asked if we *might* go.

2. Gerunds are words or phrases that have verbs as the root and *ing* endings. Though formed from verbs they act as nouns. When a gerund is preceded by a noun or a pronoun, the noun or pronoun must take the possessive form.

   I do not like *your calling* me so early in the morning.
   (*Calling* is a gerund preceded by a possessive pronoun.)
   Bob's constant nagging is annoying. (*Constant nagging*
   is a gerund phrase preceded by a possessive noun.)

3. The helping verbs *shall* and *will* are commonly confused. *Shall* expresses the future tense when used for the first person, singular and plural. *Will* expresses the future tense when used for the second and third persons, singular and plural.

   I *shall call* you in the morning.
   You *will call* me in the morning.

4. The verb *were* is often used to express wishful thinking or an idea that is contrary to the fact. *Was*, on the other hand, is used to express a statement of fact or possible fact.

   I wish I *were* a millionaire. (wishful thinking)
   She acts as if she *were* president of the company.
      (contrary to fact)
   If Jack *was* at the airport, I did not see him. (a possible
      fact)

5. *Should* denotes a duty or an obligation. *Would* denotes a condition or state of being; it is also used to express habitual behavior.

   Our company *should* have the proposal ready by the
      tenth. (obligation)
   Our company *would* be pleased to have the proposal
      ready by the tenth. (condition)
   As a boy he *would* always be tinkering with some-
      thing. (habitual behavior)

6. When using the infinitive form of the verb (the present tense preceded by *to*), do not split the infinitive with a modifier.

Right: The company president wants *to review* the proposal *carefully* before rendering a decision.

Wrong: The company president wants *to carefully review* the proposal before rendering a decision.

Super Stumpers

Lie and *lay*, *sit* and *set*, and *rise* and *raise* are three commonly misused pairs of verbs. They are conjugated as follows:

Present	Past	Perfect
lie	lay	lain
lay	laid	laid
sit	sat	sat
set	set	set
rise	rose	risen
raise	raised	raised

The first verb of each pair (*lie, sit, rise*) does not have an object. In relation to these verbs, you cannot answer the questions: What? Whom? The second verb of each pair (*lay, set, raise*) does have an object. You can answer the questions: What? Whom?

The new building will *lie* between Madison and Fifth avenues. (lie what or whom? not answered)
Please *lay* the book on the desk. (lay what? the book)
I would like to *sit* at the second table. (sit what or whom? not answered)

The man did not know how to *set* the alarm. (set
what? the alarm)

The bread will *rise* at a warm temperature. (rise what
or whom? not answered)

Raise your glass and toast the new year. (raise what?
your glass)

Note that the past tense of *lie* is *lay*, which does not have
an object.

Yesterday I was so tired that I *lay* down for an hour.

Subject and Verb Agreement

One of the most basic rules of grammar is that the subject
and the verb must agree in number. The third-person singular
verb ends in *s*. The plural is the same for all persons.

Third-Person Singular	All Plurals
is	are
was	were
has	have
gets	get
tells	tell

The boy *was* there early.
The boys *were* there early.
She *is* aware of the situation.
They *are* aware of the situation.

1. *Many a, many an,* and *each and every* always require a
   singular verb.

   Each and every typewriter *is* needed for the project.
   Many a man *has* been denied the opportunity.

2. *None, some, any, all, most,* and fractions are either singular or plural, depending on the noun they modify.

   Half of the *shipment has* been misplaced. (The subject, *shipment,* is singular.)
   Half of the *boxes have* been misplaced. (The subject, *boxes,* is plural.)

3. When referring to the name of a book, magazine, song, company, or article, use a singular verb even though the name itself may be plural.

   Little Women is one of the great classics.
   Greenberg & Wanderman is a fine team of attorneys.

4. When referring to an amount, money, distance, etc., use a singular verb if the noun is thought of as a single unit.

   I feel that *$600 is* a fair price. (a single amount)
   Six hundred books *are* located on the shelves. (individual books)

5. For an explanation of collective nouns, refer to the "Nouns" section of this chapter.

6. When *or* or *nor* is used to connect a singular and a plural subject, the verb must agree in number with the person or item closest to the verb.

   Neither the boss nor the *secretaries were* available.
   Neither the secretaries nor the *boss was* available.
   Either Bill or his *sister is* able to attend.
   Either Bill or his *sisters are* able to attend.

	PRESENT	PAST	FUTURE	PRESENT PERFECT	PAST PERFECT	FUTURE PERFECT
I	call	called	shall call	have called	had called	shall have called
you	call	called	will call	have called	had called	will have called
she he it	calls	called	will call	has called	had called	will have called
we	call	called	shall call	have called	had called	shall have called

	PRESENT	PAST	FUTURE	PRESENT PERFECT	PAST PERFECT	FUTURE PERFECT
you	call	called	will call	have called	had called	will have called
they	call	called	will call	have called	had called	will have called

CHAPTER 3

CAPITALIZATION

First Words, Calendar Dates, Seasons, Holidays, Historic Events, Commercial Products, Compass Points, Diseases, Family Relationships, Governmental Bodies, Heavenly Bodies and Supreme Beings, Hyphenated Names and Prefixes, Legal Documents, Literary Titles, Numbers and Letters with Nouns, Organizations and Institutions, Personal Names and Titles, Proper and Common Nouns, School Subjects

First Words

1. Always capitalize the first words of (a) a complete sentence, (b) a direct quotation that is a complete sentence, and (c) a complete sentence that follows a colon.

   The passenger gave the taxi driver a large tip.
   He said, "Have a wonderful time this evening."
   The sign reads: Keep off the grass.

2. Always capitalize the first word in each line of a poem.

THE LULLABY
The room is shadowed by twilight falling,
And in the silence a voice is calling,
A mother is singing her young one to sleep,
Singing a "lullaby from the deep"...

by Ethel Lorenz

3. Capitalize the major words of the salutation and first word of a complimentary closing of a letter.

Dear Mr. Fredericks:	Sincerely yours,
Gentlemen:	Very truly yours,
Dear Sir:	Yours truly,
Dear Judge Triolo:	Respectfully yours,

Calendar Dates, Seasons, Holidays, Historic Events

4. Always capitalize the names of holidays, days of the week, months of the year, historic events, holidays, and specific periods of time.

Thanksgiving	Memorial Day
Wednesday	February
the Renaissance	the McCarthy Era
D-Day	the Civil War

5. Do not capitalize the seasons of the year unless the season is being personified (given human characteristics).

Before Old Man Winter approaches, we should put on our winter snow tires.

Commercial Products

6. Always capitalize the brand or trade name but not the noun that it identifies.

Del Monte catsup	Parker pen
Coke	Savarin coffee
Chevrolet automobile	Arrow shirts
Dial soap	Timex watches

7. Do not capitalize terms that derive from proper nouns if they are no longer associated with their origin and are used as common nouns.

italian dressing	chauvinist
china (dishes)	french fries
turkish towels	roman numerals
escalator	watt

Compass Points

8. Points on the compass (north, south, east, and west) and their derivatives are capitalized only when they refer to a major region, not a direction, or are part of a place name.

I plan to take a trip out West. (major region)
He was traveling east on Route 17 when the accident occurred. (direction)
Their address is 205 West Maple Avenue. (part of an address)

I plan to visit the *Far East* and the *Middle East*. (derivatives used for major regions)

9. The adjectives *northern, southern, eastern,* and *western* are capitalized when they are part of a proper name.

   southern Jersey   Eastern Seaboard
   Western Hemisphere   Northern Ireland

Diseases

10. Capitalize the name of a disease when it is the name of an individual.

    Parkinson's disease   Hodgkin's disease
    measles   virus

Family Relationships

11. Capitalize family titles if they are followed by the person's name or when used alone as a title.

    I am so excited because Uncle Bob and Aunt Elsie are coming.
    I would love for Grandma to knit me a red sweater.

12. Do not capitalize family titles if they are preceded by possessive pronouns, unless they are followed immediately by a proper name.

    My mother and my uncle had a long conversation.
    My mother and my Uncle Ben had a long conversation.

Governmental Bodies and Titles

13. Always capitalize governmental bodies and high-ranking
    government officials if they are specifically designated.

>   the Senate   the Supreme Court
>   the Congress   Federal Bureau of Investigation
>   the Army   Department of the Interior
>   the Cabinet   the United Nations

The President is entertaining a foreign dignitary.
The Constitution mandates that a presidential can-
    didate must be native born and at least thirty-five
    years of age.
This year we will elect a new senator. (not specified)
The newly elected Senator Smith is currently in
    Washington. (specific)

Heavenly Bodies and Supreme Beings

14. Always capitalize the names of astronomical bodies such
    as planets, stars, and constellations. Exceptions are *sun*
    and *moon*. Names for supreme beings are capitalized, as
    are many religious terms.

>   Libra   Allah
>   God   the Lord
>   the Bible   Ten Commandments
>   Earth   the Milky Way

Hyphenated Names and Prefixes

15. Hyphenated names are capitalized as if no hyphen were
    present.

Spanish-American	Eighty-first Congress
Dallas–Forth Worth	Merriam-Webster
area	dictionaries

16. Hyphenated prefixes are not capitalized, unless the sentence begins with the hyphenated word.

Ex-President Ford is in Aspen, Colorado.
We saw ex-President Ford in Aspen, Colorado.

Legal Documents

17. In legal documents, the names attributed to the parties are always capitalized.

The Landlord agrees to supply the Tenant with gas, electricity, and water at no charge to the Tenant.

18. Special introductory phrases, also usually appearing in legal documents, are always in complete capital letters.

IN WITNESS WHEREOF, the parties...
KNOW ALL MEN BY THESE PRESENTS:
WHEREFORE, the undersigned...
IT IS HEREBY STIPULATED that...

Literary Titles

19. Always capitalize the titles of literary works and articles or chapters appearing within these works. Omit the capitalization of articles, conjunctions, and prepositions unless they start or end the title.

The New York Times or THE NEW YORK TIMES
"How to Winterize Your Home" (article)
Collier's Encyclopedia or COLLIER'S ENCYCLO-
    PEDIA

Books, magazines, newspapers, historical documents, pamphlets, brochures, movies, etc., will be either underscored or in all capital letters. Articles, names of chapters, and other parts within these writings are enclosed in quotation marks.

Numbers and Letters with Nouns

20. Always capitalize a noun that is followed by a number or letter used to identify it. The exceptions are lines, pages, paragraphs, sizes, notes, and verses.

Room 204	page 2
Policy No. 14677868	Appendix A
Catalog No. 25	Lot 3, Tract 123
Invoice No. 1234	size 10
Chapter X	Exhibit A

It is often necessary to use *No.* before the actual number. Do not use the number sign (#) in formal writing.

21. When the noun and the number are separated in the sentence, do not capitalize the descriptive word.

    I believe that 204 is the room where the meeting will
    be held.

Organizations and Institutions

22. Always capitalize the major words in the names of institutions, banks, colleges, universities, religious bodies, schools, hospitals, clubs, political parties, societies, etc.

the Republican party	New York Public Library
the Ford Foundation	the League of Women Voters
the Salvation Army	Congregation Sons of Israel
State University of New York	St. Luke's Hospital

23. Do not capitalize any of the above terms when they are used as common nouns.

    In the fall, I will apply to several *foundations*.
    I must do research at the *library*.

Personal Names and Titles

24. Capitalize all titles that precede a personal name.

General Eisenhower	Dr. Gorelick
President Jameson	Mayor-elect Smith
Ambassador Jones	Vice-President Sheridan

25. Do not capitalize titles that are used in apposition and are set off by commas unless you are referring to a high-ranking public dignitary or high-ranking member of your organization.

    Mike Fauci, *sales representative,* is scheduled to return to the office tomorrow.

The President of our company, Judy Barash, will preside at the meeting.

26. Treat the spelling of a person's name exactly as the person does. There are instances when a last name may not start with a capital letter or may have an unusual spelling. Check the telephone directory or the person's letterhead.

     John Smythe   José deLa Cruz
     Evan von Poshe   Ellen and Lucy d'Meglia

Proper and Common Nouns

27. Always capitalize a proper noun (a specific person, place, or thing). Do not capitalize a common noun (a general person, place, or thing).

Common	Proper
state	California
company	International Business Machines
book	GIFTS FROM THE SEA
language	French
holiday	Christmas
school	Taylor Business Institute
building	Empire State Building

     I am interested in purchasing the building across the street.
     The view from the Chrysler Building is breathtaking.

28. Always capitalize a nickname that commonly substitutes for the real name.

     the Bay Area (San Francisco)
     the Big Board (New York Stock Exchange)

Big D (Dallas)
the Big Apple (New York City)

29. Always capitalize nationalities and races (with the exception of *black* and *white*).

> Caucasian   African-American
> Indian   Japanese

30. Always capitalize the names of continents, nations, states, cities, towns, bodies of water, avenues, harbors, etc.

> New York State   Fifth Avenue
> New England   Atlantic Ocean

Do not capitalize a geographical term that precedes a name unless it is a designated part of that name.

I had a wonderful visit to the city of Miami.
New York City has so much to offer.

31. Do not capitalize a plural noun that describes two or more proper nouns.

Meet me at the corner of Main and Troy streets.
I have seen the Appalachian and Rocky mountains.

School Subjects

32. Capitalize the names of courses when they refer to specific courses or are the names of languages.

> Typewriting 102   Spanish

CHAPTER 4

NUMBERS

Basic Rules, Addresses, Adjacent Numbers, Amounts of Money, Beginning Sentences, Book Divisions, Centuries and Decades, Dates, Decimals, Dimensions, Degrees, Fractions and Mixed Numbers, Hours of the Day, Hyphenated Numbers, Ordinals, Millions and Above, Percentages, Weights and Measures, Numbers in Columns

Basic Rules

1. Numbers from one to ten are generally written as words, and numbers above ten are generally written as figures. This rule applies to exact numbers and approximations.

   Only five people volunteered to help.
   There were 20 people who volunteered to help.
   Approximately 50,000 tickets were sold for the concert.
   About ten cartons should be sufficient.

2. Numbers in a sentence that perform the same function should be written uniformly. If one is written as a figure, all should be expressed as figures.

We completed only 9 of the 12 projects.
We ordered 3 desks, 3 chairs, and 15 lighting fixtures.
She bought four 75-watt bulbs. (different functions)

Addresses

3. Use figures to represent a house or building number, with the exception of *one*, which should be spelled out.

   He resides at One Park Place.
   He resides at 2 Park Place.

Adjacent Numbers

4. When two unrelated numbers are written together, generally write one as figures and the other as words. The one in words should be the shorter of the two. If both are too large to be written in words, write both as figures and use a comma to separate them. If both are written as words, also use a comma to separate them.

   We had two $100 bills.
   The landlord owns two 6-room homes.
   In 1970, 315 of the company's employees moved to Atlanta.
   Of the three, two qualified.

Amounts of Money

5. Figures are used to represent exact amounts of money. The dollar sign ($) is placed immediately before the num-

ber and no ciphers (.00) are used when expressing even dollar amounts.

A balance of $350.50 remains in our treasury.
A balance of $350 remains in our treasury.

6. For amounts less than a dollar, the word *cents* follows the number.

He received only 45 cents in change.

7. Indefinite amounts of money are generally spelled out.

A few million dollars will be needed to complete the project.
Many hundreds of dollars need to be raised by June.

8. For uniformity and clarity, use the dollar sign with amounts under a dollar in a series of related numbers when dollars and cents are mixed.

The young child received the following amounts of money by selling lemonade: $1.50, $2.00, and $.95.

9. Money representing a million dollars or more should be expressed as follows:

A $3.5 million budget has recently been approved.

10. If the million dollar figure consists of more than a whole number and simple fractional amount, use figures.

The company realized a profit of $3,245,000 last year.

Beginning Sentences

11. When a number begins a sentence, the number must be written as words. If the number is too long, it may be necessary to reword the sentence.

    Right: Thirty-five people were injured in the fire.
    Wrong: 35 people were injured in the fire.
    Right: In 1979 we had our best year.
    Wrong: 1979 was our best year.

Book Divisions

12. Pages and divisions of a book are referred to in figures. For capitalization, see Rule 20 of the "Capitalization" chapter.

    The information appears in Volume X, Chapter 3, page 3, line 2 of the book we just discussed.

Centuries and Decades

13. Centuries and decades may be expressed in either of the styles shown below. Decades are not capitalized except in such expressions as the *Roaring Twenties*.

    Our company was founded in the early 1900s. (1900's)
    Our company was founded in the early nineteen hundreds.
    The twentieth century has shown more progress than any other.

Dates

14. When the day follows the month, use figures only.

   The meeting was tentatively scheduled for May 1,
   19XX.
   The draft must be submitted no later than June 1.
   (not *June 1st* or *June first*)

NOTE: Check "Addresses and Dates" in the comma section
of the "Punctuation" chapter for comma rules governing dates.

15. When the day stands alone or precedes the month, it may
   be expressed in ordinal figures or in ordinal words, depending on the degree of emphasis indicated.

   The meeting is tentatively scheduled for the 1st of
   May.
   The meeting is tentatively scheduled for the first of
   May.
   I plan to arrive on the tenth; can you meet me?

   In formal writing, always spell out the names of months.
   (not *Mar. 1, 1989* or *3/1/89*)

16. In military or foreign correspondence the date is frequently
   written as follows:

                   22 September 19XX

17. In very formal documents, both the day and the year are
   spelled out.

   on the sixteenth of September, in the year of Our
   Lord one thousand nine hundred eighty-two

Decimals, Dimensions, Degrees

18. Decimals are always written as figures with no comma separation to the right of the decimal.

    25.5678 (no comma separation to the right)
    8,543.5678 (comma separation to the left)

19. Dimensions are always written as figures.

    The rug measures 9 by 12 feet.
    The rug measures 9 × 12 feet.

20. Degrees are always written as figures with either the word *degree* or the degree symbol (°).

    The temperature is a blustery 22 degrees below zero.
    The temperature is a blustery 22° below zero.

Fractions and Mixed Numbers

21. Fractions not expressed with whole numbers are written as words.

    By the time I arrived home, three-fourths of the pie had been eaten. (Always separate the numerator from the denominator with a hyphen.)

22. Fractions expressed with whole numbers are written as figures.

    The runner had to complete an additional 3-3/4 miles.

Hours of the Day

23. Hours of the day are expressed as figures when *a.m.* or *p.m.* (AM or PM) follow. When no minutes are indicated, the ciphers (:00) should not be used.

    My train will arrive at 9:15 a.m.
    My train will arrive at 9 p.m.

    The ciphers should be used, however, to create uniformity in related hours.

    My train will arrive between 9:00 and 9:15 p.m.

24. When the hours of the day are not followed by a.m. or p.m. but by the word *o'clock*, either figures or words may be used.

    ten o'clock   10 o'clock

25. The words *noon* and *midnight* are used to express the 12 o'clock hours.

    I can meet you for lunch at 12 noon.
    I must arrive home no later than 12 midnight.

Hyphenated Numbers

26. The compound numbers 21 to 99 are always hyphenated when written as words.

    Twenty-one people attended the party.
    One hundred fifty-two people attended the party.

27. A hyphen may be used to represent numbers in a continuous series.

    Please read pages 205-215.
    He served one term, 1976-1979. (not *from 1976-1979*)

Ordinals

28. Ordinal figures used with names are expressed in any of the following ways with no period following.

    Thomas James Lindsell 2nd
    Thomas James Lindsell 2d
    Thomas James Lindsell II
    Thomas James Lindsell, Jr. (When *Jr.* is used in place of the ordinal, a comma precedes it.)

Millions and Above

29. Any number of a million or more is treated as indicated for money amounts in Rules 15 and 16.

    The winner of the congressional race received more than 2.5 million votes.
    The candidate received 2,560,000 votes.

Percentages

30. Percentages are written as figures followed by the word *percent* unless beginning a sentence.

    Only 25 percent of the votes were counted.
    Twenty-five percent of the votes were counted.

31. Fractional percentages may be expressed as follows:

    one-fourth of one percent   .25 percent

32. When a hyphen is used to connect percentages, the word *percent* should be placed after the last amount. When the percent symbol (%) is used, it must follow each figure.

    The candidate received 25–30 percent of the votes.
    The invoice indicated a 2% or 3% discount.

Weights and Measures

33. Dimensions, weights, distances, measurements, etc. should be written as figures followed by the spelled-out version of the unit or measurement.

    The basketball player stood 7 feet 5 inches tall.
    The package weighs 5 pounds 10 ounces.

    Note that no commas are used to separate these units.

Numbers in Columns

34. Numbers listed in a column should always be justified (lined up) at the right.

$$
\begin{array}{r}
200 \\
1,500 \\
6 \\
17,567 \\
25
\end{array}
$$

CHAPTER 5

WORD DIVISION

A word divided incorrectly is a misspelled word. Consult your dictionary when in doubt, and adhere to the following rules.

DON'TS

1. Do not use excessive word division.
2. Do not divide a word in the first line or last line on a page.
3. Do not divide a word in the first line of a paragraph.
4. Do not divide a one-syllable word, no matter how long the word may be. (*length, brought, straight*)
5. Do not divide words on two consecutive lines.
6. Do not divide a proper name or number. (*Washington, $153.69*)
7. Do not separate one or two letters from the rest of the word. (*acute, overall, reward, heater, shovel*)
8. Do not separate contractions or abbreviations. (*shouldn't, NATO, ASPCA*)

DO'S

1. A word should be divided only between syllables. Dic-

tionaries indicate syllabication by the use of a bold •, but rely on your rules also.

com•fort   pro•ce•dure

2. A word should be divided only if it contains six letters or more.

inept   pre•pare

3. If a vowel stands alone as a single syllable, it must remain on the same line as the first part of the word.

experi•ment   mini•mum

4. Divide between double consonants.

admis•sion   bat•tery
cud•dle   neces•sary

Exception: Do not divide a word between double consonants if it means breaking up the root of the word.

pass•ing   install•ing

5. If a word contains a natural hyphen, divide only at that point.

self-determination   fifty-six
two-thirds

6. If a word contains a prefix or suffix, it is best to divide at that point.

establish•ment   dis•appear
draw•ing   pre•determine

CHAPTER 6

SPELLING

Doubling the Final Consonants, The Final e, *The Final* y, ie *and* ei, *Plurals*

Spelling Motto: *If in doubt, check it out!*

The common outcry of employers is "My secretary cannot spell." If you produce a masterpiece of typing and it contains a spelling error, what do you think will be remembered? Your error.

Your dictionary can be one of your most valuable reference guides, but you should make a list of words with which you have difficulty and which are used frequently in your particular company or industry. Don't waste time constantly checking your dictionary; your own word list together with a knowledge of the rules of spelling will aid you in overcoming many of the spelling difficulties you may have.

NOTE: There are exceptions to every rule.

Doubling the Final Consonant

Double the final consonant before a suffix if:

1. It is a one-syllable word or has its accent on the last syllable.

hop	hopped	hopping
commit	committed	committing
plan	planned	planning
defer	deferred	deferring
omit	omitted	omitting

2. It is a word ending in a single vowel followed by a single consonant.

occur	occurred	occurring
transfer	transferred	transferring
prefer	preferred	preferring
infer	inferred	inferring
permit	permitted	permitting
allot	allotted	allotting

The Final e

Drop the final *e* preceded by a consonant before a suffix that starts with a vowel.

excuse + able = excusable
like + able = likable
obese + ity = obesity
entitle + ing = entitling
argue + ing = arguing
desire + ous = desirous
(Common exceptions: changeable, noticeable, courageous)

Retain the final *e* when the suffix begins with a consonant.

move + ment = movement
strange + ly = strangely

appropriate + ly = appropriately
state + ment = statement
care + less = careless
resource + ful = resourceful

The Final y

Retain the final y when it is preceded by a vowel.

attorney + s = attorneys
annoy + ed = annoyed
buy + er = buyer
journey + s = journeys
employ + ers = employers
annoy + ance = annoyance

Change the final y to an *i* when it is preceded by a consonant.

salary + es = salaries
reply + ed = replied
beauty + ful = beautiful
angry + ly = angrily
cozy + ness = coziness
easy + ly = easily

ie and ei

Put *i* before *e*, (fiend, yield)
Except after *c*, (receive, conceit)
Or when sounded like *a*,
As in *neighbor* and *weigh*;
And except *seize* and *seizure*,
And also *leisure*,

Weird, height, and *either,*
Forfeit and *neither.*

handkerchief	deceit
client	surveillance
niece	heir

Plurals

The plurals of most nouns are formed by the addition of *s*.

cat + s = cats
automobile + s = automobiles
hand + s = hands
typewriter + s = typewriters
tree + s = trees
employee + s = employees

Words ending in *s*, *x*, *z*, *ch*, or *sh* are made plural by the addition of *es*.

business + es = businesses
catch + es = catches
Jones + es = Joneses
Sanchez + es = Sanchezes
tax + es = taxes
box + es = boxes

Words ending in *y* that are preceded by a vowel are made plural by the addition of an *s*.

key + s = keys
journey + s = journeys
alley + s = alleys
turkey + s = turkeys
attorney + s = attorneys

chimney + s = chimneys

Words ending in *y* that are preceded by a consonant are made plural by changing the *y* to *i* and adding *es*.

academy + es = academies
secretary + es = secretaries
company + es = companies
cry + es = cries
army + es = armies
beneficiary + es = beneficiaries

Exception: When a person's name ends in *y* and is preceded by a consonant, it is made plural by the addition of an *s*. Otherwise it would be unclear, in some cases, whether the name ends in *y* or *i*.

Kennedy + s = Kennedys
Mary + s = Marys
Pokarsky + s = Pokarskys

Words ending in *o* that are preceded by a vowel are generally made plural by the addition of an *s*.

studio + s = studios
radio + s = radios

Most words ending in *o* that are preceded by a consonant are made plural by the addition of *es*; however, some require only an *s*. If in doubt, check it out!

veto + es = vetoes
echo + es = echoes
hero + es = heroes

Musical terms ending in *o* are made plural by the addition of an *s*.

piano + s = pianos

```
soprano + s = sopranos
banjo + s = banjos
solo + s = solos
```

Some words are made plural by changing the vowel and/or the form.

man	men
mouse	mice
child	children
tooth	teeth
Mr.	Messrs. (from French)
Mrs.	Mmes. (from French)
ox	oxen

Some words are the same in the singular and plural forms.

deer	deer
news	news
mathematics	mathematics
economics	economics
series	series
sheep	sheep

In a hyphenated compound word, the principal part of the word will be made plural.

brother-in-law	brothers-in-law
sister-in-law	sisters-in-law
editor-in-chief	editors-in-chief

In a compound word that is not hyphenated, the s is added at the end.

cupful	cupfuls
handful	handfuls
letterhead	letterheads

Some words that end in *f* or *fe* are made plural by changing the *f* to a *v* and adding *s* or *es*.

knife + s = knives
shelf + s = shelves
life + s = lives
wife + s = wives

Letters, signs, and figures are made plural by the addition of apostrophe *s*.

Always dot your *i*'s and cross your *t*'s.
Your 6's are not too clear; they took like O's.
Four R.N.'s applied for the nursing position.

A contraction is made plural by the addition of an *s*.

don'ts   can'ts

Many borrowed foreign words are made plural by changing the ending.

sis to *ses*:	analysis	analyses
	crisis	crises
	oasis	oases
um to *a*:	datum	data
	addendum	addenda
	memorandum	memoranda (memorandums)
us to *i*:	cactus	cacti
	radius	radii
	criterion	criteria
on to *a*:	criterion	criteria
	phenomenon	phenomena

CHAPTER 7

COMPOUND WORDS

General Rules; Solid Compounds; Unit Modifiers; Prefixes, Suffixes, and Combining Forms; Numerical, Scientific, and Technical Compounds; Improvised Compounds

A compound is a union of two or more words; it conveys a unit idea that is not as clearly or quickly conveyed by the component words in unconnected succession. Compounds may be spelled open (with a space), solid (with no space), or with a hyphen.

General Rules

1. In general, omit the hyphen when words appear in regular order and the omission causes no ambiguity in sense or sound. (See also rule 13.)

banking hours	eye opener	real estate
blood pressure	fellow citizen	rock candy
book value	living costs	training ship
census taker	palm oil	violin teacher
day laborer	patent right	

2. Words are usually combined to express a literal or nonliteral (figurative) unit idea that would not be as clearly expressed in unconnected succession.

afterglow	forget-me-not	right-of-way
bookkeeping	gentleman	whitewash

3. Unless otherwise indicated, a derivative of a compound retains the solid or hyphenated form of the original compound.

coldbloodedness	praiseworthiness
footnoting	railroader
ill-advisedly	Y-shaped

4. Except after the short prefixes *co, de, pre, pro,* and *re,* which are generally typed solid, a hyphen is used to avoid doubling a vowel or tripling a consonant.

cooperation	Inverness-shire
preexisting	thimble-eye
anti-inflation	ultra-atomic
semi-independent	shell-like

Solid Compounds

5. Type solid two nouns that form a third when the compound has only one primary accent, especially when the prefixed noun consists of only one syllable or when one of the elements loses its original accent.

airship	cupboard	footnote
bathroom	dressmaker	locksmith

6. Type solid a noun consisting of a short verb and an adverb as its second element, except when the use of the solid form would interfere with comprehension.

blowout	runoff
breakdown	*but* run-in
pickup	

7. Compounds beginning with the following nouns are usually typed solid.

book	mill	snow
eye	play	way
horse	school	wood
house	shop	work

8. Compounds ending in the following are usually typed solid, especially when the prefixed word consists of one syllable.

berry	maker	tight
blossom	making	time
boat	man	ward
book	master	way
borne	mate	weed
bound	mill	wide
brained	mistress	wise
bush	monger	woman
fish	owner	wood
flower	piece	work
grower	power	worker
hearted	proof	working
holder	room	worm
house	shop	wort
keeper	smith	writer
keeping	stone	writing
light	store	yard
like	tail	

9. Type solid *any*, *every*, *no*, and *some* when combined with *body*, *thing*, and *where*; when *one* is the second element, print as two words if meaning a single or particular person or thing; to avoid mispronunciation, print *no one* as two words at all times.

anybody	nobody
anything	nothing
anywhere	nowhere
anyone	no one
everybody	somebody

but Any one of us may stay.

Every one of the pilots is responsible.

10. Type as one word compound personal pronouns.

herself	oneself	itself
himself	ourselves	yourself

11. Type as one word compass directions consisting of two points, but use a hyphen after the first point when three points are combined.

northeast	north-northwest
southwest	south-southeast

Unit Modifiers

12. Except as indicated in the other rules in this chapter, type a hyphen between words, or abbreviations and words, combined to form a unit modifier immediately preceding the word modified. This applies particularly to combinations in which the second element is a present or past participle.

Baltimore-Washington road
drought-stricken area

English-speaking nation
Federal-State-local cooperation
fire-tested material
German-English descent
high-speed line
large-scale project
law-abiding citizen
long-term loan
long-term-payment loan
lump-sum payment
most-favored-nation clause
multiple-purpose uses
no-par-value stock
part-time personnel
rust-resistant covering
service-connected disability
tool-and-die maker
two-inch-diameter pipe
ten-word telegram

13. Where the meaning is clear and readability is not aided, it is not necessary to use a hyphen to form a temporary or made compound. Restraint should be exercised in forming unnecessary combinations of words used in normal sequence.

atomic energy power
child welfare plan
civil rights case
civil service examination
durable goods industry
flood control study
free enterprise system
high school student; elementary school grade

income tax form
interstate commerce law
land use program
life insurance company
mutual security funds
national defense appropriation
natural gas company
per capita expenditure
product utility plant
real estate tax
small businessperson
Social Security pension
soil conservation measures
special delivery mail; parcel post delivery
but no-hyphen rule (readability aided); *not* no hyphen rule

14. When the second element is a present or past participle and the unit modifier does not immediately precede the thing modified, omit the hyphen.

   The effects were far reaching.
   The shale was oil bearing.
   The area is drought stricken.

15. Type without a hyphen a two-word modifier when the first element is a comparative or superlative.

   better drained soil
   best liked books
   larger sized dress
   better paying job
   lower income group
   but uppercrust society
        lowercase, uppercase type (printing)
        bestseller (noun)
        lighter-than-air craft
        higher-than-market price

16. Do not use a hyphen in a two-word unit modifier when the first element is an adverb ending in -ly.

    eagerly awaited moment
    wholly owned subsidiary

17. Proper nouns used as unit modifiers—either in their basic or derived form—retain their original form, but the hyphen is typed after combining forms.

    Latin American countries
    North Carolina roads
    a Mexican American
    South American trade
    Winston-Salem festival
    Washington-Wilkes-Barre route
    African-American program
    Anglo-Saxon period
    Minneapolis-St. Paul region

18. Do not confuse a modifier with the word it modifies.

    prudent stockholder
    canning factory
    light blue hat
    average taxpayer
    American flagship
    but common-stock holder
        tomato-canning factory
        light-blue hat
        income-tax payer
        American-flag ship

19. Where two or more hyphenated compounds have a common basic element and this element is omitted in all but the last term, the hyphens are retained.

two- to three-ton trucks

8-, 10-, and 16-foot boards

moss- and ivy-covered walls, *not* moss and ivy-covered walls

long- and short-term money rates, *not* long and short-term money rates

but twofold or threefold, *not* two or threefold

    goat, sheep, and calf skins, *not* goat, sheep, and calf-skins

    American owned and managed companies

20. Omit the hyphen in a unit modifier containing a letter or numeral as its second element.

abstract B pages	grade A milk
article 3 provisions	class II railroad

Prefixes, Suffixes, and Combining Forms

21. Compounds formed with prefixes and suffixes are typed solid, except as indicated elsewhere.

*after*birth	*in*bound	*post*script
*Anglo*mania	*infra*red	*pre*exist
*ante*date	*inter*view	*pseudo*science
*anti*slavery	*intro*vert	*re*enact
*bi*weekly	*iso*metric	*retro*spect
*by*law	*macro*analysis	*semi*official
*circum*navigation	*micro*phone	*step*father
*co*operate	*mis*state	*sub*secretary
*contra*position	*mono*gram	*super*market
*de*energize	*multi*color	*trans*ship
*demi*tasse	*neo*phyte	*tri*color
*ex*communicate	*non*neutral	*ultra*violet

*extra*curricular	*off*set	*un*necessary
*fore*tell	*over*active	
*hyper*sensitive	*peri*patetic	

port*able*	ge*ography*	partner*ship*
cover*age*	sel*fish*	lone*some*
oper*ate*	meat*less*	home*stead*
plebis*cite*	out*let*	north*ward*
twenty*fold*	wave*like*	clock*wise*
spoon*ful*	procure*ment*	
kilo*gram*	inner*most*	

22. Print solid words ending in *like*, but use a hyphen to avoid tripling a consonant or when the first element is a proper name.

    lifelike   bell-like   Florida-like

23. Use a hyphen or hyphens to prevent mispronunciation, to insure a definite accent on each element of the compound, or to avoid ambiguity.

    anti-hog-cholera serum   re-cover (cover again)
    co-op   re-sort (sort again)
    mid-ice   re-treat (treat again)
    non-civil-service position   un-ionized

24. Type with a hyphen the prefixes *ex*, *self*, and *quasi*.

    ex-governor   *but* selfhood
    ex-vice-president   selfsame
    self-control   quasi-academic
    self-educated   quasi-argument

25. Unless usage demands otherwise, use a hyphen to join a prefix or combining form to a capitalized word. (The hyphen is retained in words of this class set in caps.)

anti-Arab   pro-British
un-American   *but* nongovernmental
non-Government   transatlantic

26. The adjectives *elect* and *designate*, as the last element of a title, require a hyphen.

President-elect   ambassador-designate

Numerical, Scientific, and Technical Compounds

27. Do not type a hyphen in scientific terms (names of chemicals, diseases, animals, insects, plants) used as unit modifiers if no hyphen appears in their original form.

carbon monoxide poisoning
guinea pig raising
hog cholera serum
methyl bromide solution
stem rust control
equivalent uranium content
whooping cough remedy
but screw-worm raising
        Russian-olive plantings
        white-pine weevil
        Douglas-fir tree

28. Chemical elements used in combination with figures use a hyphen, except with superior figures.

polonium-210
uranium-235; *but* U^{225}; Sr^{90}; 92^{U234}
Freon-12

29. Note use of hyphens and closeup punctuation in chemical formulas.

    9-nitroanthra (1,9,4,10)   bis(1)oxathiazone-2,7-bis
    dioxide Cr-NI-Mo
    2,4-D

30. Print a hyphen between the elements of technical compound units of measurement.

    candle-hour   light-year
    horsepower-hour   passenger-mile
    kilowatt-hour

Improvised Compounds

31. Type with a hyphen the elements of an improvised compound.

    blue-pencil (v.)
    18-year-old (n.)
    first-come-first-served basis
    know-it-all (n.)
    know-how (n.)
    make-believe (n.)
    one-man-one-vote principle
    stick-in-the-mud (n.)
    let-George-do-it attitude
    how-to-be-beautiful course
    hard-and-fast rule
    penny-wise and pound-foolish policy
    but a basis of first come, first served
         easy come, easy go

32. Use a hyphen to join a single capital letter to a noun or participle.

H-bomb   X-raying
I-beam   T-shaped
V-necked   U-boat

CHAPTER 8

COMMONLY CONFUSED WORDS

accede (v)   to yield, assent
exceed (v)   to surpass or go beyond

> The smaller nation will *accede* to the conquering larger nation.
>
> He *exceeded* all expectations.

accept (v)   to take or receive
except (prep)   other than

> Please *accept* my apology.
>
> No one will understand *except* Thomas.

access (n)   right to enter, admittance
assess (v)   set a value
excess (n)   extra or surplus
   (adj)   extra or surplus

> Please grant Mr. Feiler *access* to the files.
>
> We will *assess* the situation at a later date.
>
> This *excess* in spending can no longer be tolerated.
>
> The *excess* paper will be collected tomorrow.

| ad (n) | short for *advertisement* |
| add (v) | to increase, unite, or combine |

I saw your *ad* in yesterday's newspaper.
Please *add* this book to your collection.

adapt (v)	to adjust, make fit
adept (adj)	skilled or expert at
adopt (v)	take as your own, accept, choose

You must learn to *adapt* to various climates.
He is a highly *adept* swimmer.
The corporation will *adopt* new bylaws.

| addenda (n) | (plural of *addendum*) something added |
| agenda (n) | program of things to be done |

The attorney added two *addenda* to the contract.
Please put Mr. Teisch on the *agenda* for tomorrow.

| addition (n) | something added |
| edition (n) | published work |

Janice is a welcome *addition* to our staff.
The new *edition* will be published next month.

| adverse (adj) | hostile, opposite in direction, unfavorable |
| averse (adj) | unwilling, disinclined |

The *adverse* weather conditions caused many hardships.
I would not be *averse* to your suggestions.

| advice (n) | an opinion, counsel, recommendation |
| advise (v) | to give an opinion, to counsel |

This is very sound *advice*.
Please *advise* me if the situation changes.

affect (v)	to influence
effect (n)	result
(v)	to bring about, accomplish

Your attitude will *affect* your performance.
What *effect* did Mr. Sullivan's actions have on you?
You can *effect* many changes if you persevere.

air (n)	atmosphere
heir (n)	person who inherits

The *air* quality today is favorable.
The *heir* to the estate is Jackie Lorenz.

aisle (n)	passageway
isle (n)	island
I'll (contraction)	I shall

The *aisles* in the theater are very narrow.
The British *Isles* are very beautiful.
I'll see you tomorrow evening.

allowed (v)	past tense of *allow*
aloud (adv)	loudly, audibly

They will be *allowed* to tour the factory tomorrow.
Please speak *aloud*.

allusion (n)	indirect reference, casual mention
illusion (n)	false idea or impression
elusion (n)	escape, avoidance
delusion (n)	false belief

His *allusion* to their meeting was unintentional.
An optical *illusion* was created by the mirror.
His *elusion* of the police baffled everyone.
Napoleon suffered from *delusions* of grandeur.

already (adv/adj)	previously
all ready* (adj)	all prepared

We were *already* introduced.
The children were *all ready* for their test.

alright	nonstandard English for *all right*
all right	entirely correct

Will it be *all right* to make the delivery in June?
Are you *all right*?

altar (n)	part of church, raised platform
alter (v)	to change

The bride and groom were married in front of the
   altar.
Do not *alter* your plans on my behalf.

alternate (v)	to substitute or take turns
(n)	a substitute
alternative (n)	one of two or more options

Please *alternate* between the odd and the even.
An *alternate* will be selected in case of illness.
Several *alternatives* must be considered.

altogether (adv)	entirely
all together* (adv)	everyone in one group

He is *altogether* too tall to be a jockey.
The family was *all together* for the reading of the will.

When the word *all* can be omitted and the sentence still makes sense, it will be the two-word version.

The papers are (*all*) *together* on my desk.

annual (adj)	yearly
annul (v)	to cancel

This magazine is an *annual* publication.
Mr. and Mrs. Feiler will not *annul* their marriage.

ante- (prefix)	before
anti- (prefix)	against

The *ante*room was beautifully decorated.
The *anti*biotic should help fight the disease.

appraise (v)	estimate or set value on
apprise (v)	notify, inform

The property was *appraised* at $40,000.
Kindly *apprise* me if his condition worsens.

are (v)	form of verb *to be*
hour (n)	period of time
our (adj)	belonging to us

There *are* many people who will believe her story.
Sam Barash seems to be busy every *hour* in the day.
Our possessions are of great value.

area (n)	place, surface, scope
aria (n)	melody
arrears (n)	being behind in obligation

The entire *area* was muddy after the rain.
The *aria* was beautifully sung.
His account is 30 days in *arrears*.

arraign (v)   to accuse, bring to court
arrange (v)   to put in order

> The accused was *arraigned* on charges of reckless driv-
> ing.
> Please *arrange* the files in numerical order.

ascent (n)   the act of rising or climbing
assent (n)   consent
       (v)   to agree to

> The mountain climber found the *ascent* to be difficult.
> The *assent* was given by the judge.
> The judge *assented* to the decision of the jury.

assistance (n)   help, aid
assistants (n)   those who help

> Any *assistance* will be greatly appreciated.
> Two *assistants* volunteered to move the furniture.

attendance (n)   act of attending, total number attend-
                          ing
attendants (n)   persons who attend

> Your *attendance* in class is required.
> The parking lot *attendants* were most helpful.

aural (adj)   relating to the ear
oral (adj)   relating to the mouth

> The *aural* infection caused his ear to swell.
> The dentist performed an *oral* examination.

bail (n)	security, release
(v)	to set free, to deliver in trust
bale (n)	a bundle

Bail was arranged for the prisoner.
He was *bailed* out of jail.
A *bale* of hay lasts only a short time.

bare (adj)	naked, no more than
bear (v)	to carry, to endure, to produce
(n)	animal

These are the *bare* facts.
She could not *bear* to leave him home.
The *bear* is shedding its fur.

base (n)	foundation
(adj)	lacking decency
bass (n)	species of fish, lowest male voice

The *base* of the building is concrete.
Because of his *base* personality, people avoided him.
They fished for *bass*.
His *bass* voice enhances the choir.

bases (n)	plural of *base* and *basis*
basis (n)	foundation, main factor

The decision was made on the *bases* of input from
both of you.
There is no solid *basis* for your decision.

bazaar (n)	marketplace
bizarre (adj)	odd, queer

The *bazaar* offered many bargains.
What a *bizarre* ending to that story.

beat (n)	tempo, series of movements
beet (n)	vegetable

The *beat* of that music is good for dancing.
The *beet* crop did not do very well with all the rain
we had.

berry (n)	small, juicy fruit
bury (v)	to hide, cover over

The *berry* had a delicious flavor.
Let's *bury* our problems and go forward.

beside (prep)	near, alongside
besides (prep)	in addition to

The plant was placed *beside* the table.
The man has two dogs *besides* Rusty.

better (adj)	comparative degree of *good*
bettor (n)	person who gambles

The apple was *better* than the pear.
The *bettor* is not always the winner.

biannual (adj)	twice a year, semiannual
biennial (adj)	every two years

Prepare for the *biannual* meeting of the board of directors.
A *biennial* planting should be sufficient.

bibliography (n)	list of sources of information
biography (n)	account of a person's life

The *bibliography* will be found at the end of the book.
Roosevelt's *biography* was of great interest to me.

birth (n)   act of bringing forth
berth (n)   a bed

> The *birth* of their child was a great joy.
> I believe the lower *berth* is reserved.

board (n)   plank, counsel, regular meals
    (v)   close up with planks, provide meals
bored (v)   penetrated, as with a drill
    (adj)   uninterested, wearied from tedium

> The *Board* will meet to discuss the new proposal.
> Room and *board* will be provided at no additional
>   charge.
> After they had *bored* through the wall, they had ven-
>   tilation.
> Marc was *bored* at the meeting; therefore, he left early.

boarder (n)   one who pays for meals and lodging
border (n)   edge or margin

> Our *boarder* will be gone during the month of July.
> The *border* on the glass is gold.

bolder (adj)   more bold or daring
boulder (n)   large rock

> Eric is *bolder* than I will ever be.
> The large *boulder* was impossible to move manually.

born   past participle of *bear*, brought forth
borne   past participle of *bear*, carried, endured

> The child was *born* on August 15.
> Jonathan has *borne* many problems during the year.

| boy (n) | male child |
| buoy (n) | a floating marker |

Michael Gasparre is the *boy* I have been telling you about.

Quickly, grab the *buoy*, and you will stay afloat.

brake (n)	device for stopping motion
(v)	to stop by using a brake
break (n)	a breach, fracture, sudden move
(v)	to breach, fracture, or divide

The *brake* is to the left of the gas pedal.

If you *brake* on ice, you may skid.

The accused made a sudden *break* for the door.

If you *break* the contract, you will be sued.

| bread (n) | food made of dough |
| bred | past participle of *breed*, brought up |

Rye *bread* is my favorite.

David Dworkin is a well-*bred* young man.

bridal (adj)	of a bride or wedding
bridle (n)	harness for a horse
(v)	to restrain

The *bridal* party was dressed in lilac.

The horse pulled at his *bridle*.

Some gossips would be wise to *bridle* their tongues.

| broach (v) | to bring up, introduce |
| brooch (n) | ornamental piece of jewelry |

I would not *broach* the subject until later.

Mrs. Teisch's *brooch* is exquisite.

| build (v) | erect or construct |
| billed | past participle of *bill*, to charge |

Mr. Sheridan will *build* his store on this site.
You will not be *billed* for the merchandise until next
month.

| buy (v) | to purchase |
| by (prep) | expressing relationship of space, time, mode |

We have become a *buy*-now-and-pay-later society.
Please have the project completed *by* noon.

| calendar (n) | a record of time |
| calender (n) | machine for processing cloth or paper |

I must get a *calendar* for the new year.
The order will be delayed because the *calender* is in
need of repair.

| cannot | correct form for *can not* |

I *cannot* see any purpose in continuing this discussion.

| canvas (n) | a coarse cloth |
| canvass (v) | to solicit |

The sailor's duffel bag was made of *canvas*.
Politicians *canvass* neighborhoods seeking votes.

capital (n)	official city of a state, money, wealth
capital (adj)	chief, serious
capitol (n)	building which houses a state legislature

| Capitol (n) | building in Washington, DC which houses Congress |

Much *capital* will be needed to start a business.
Murder is a *capital* offense.
The *capitol* in Albany is in need of repair.
When in Washington, do not miss seeing the *Capitol*.

| carton (n) | cardboard or wooden box |
| cartoon (n) | a caricature |

The large *carton* will be stored in the attic.
The *cartoon* was very funny.

| casual (adj) | not planned, random |
| causal (adj) | pertaining to a cause |

His style is extremely *casual*.
One *causal* factor of the explosion was human error.

| cease (v) | to stop |
| seize (v) | to grasp |

You are to *cease* making that noise.
The man was *seized* in the restaurant.

| cede (v) | to grant, surrender |
| seed (n) | that from which something is grown |

We are going to *cede* the adjoining property to our
   neighbor.
The *seeds* will be ready for planting in the spring.

| ceiling (n) | top of a room or limit |
| sealing (gerund) | act of closing |

The *ceiling* will be set at $2 million.
Sealing the surface will prevent leakage.

census (n)	official counting
senses (n)	(plural) feelings, reaction to stimuli
(v)	perceives, comprehends

The *census* tells of population trends.
Of all our *senses*, sight is the most acute.
The woman *senses* that something may be wrong.

cent (n)	a penny
scent (n)	odor or smell
sent (v)	past tense of *send*, dispatched

Jason spent every *cent* on the gift for his mother.
Garlic leaves a very strong *scent*.
The messenger was *sent* for the package.

cereal (n)	any grain food
serial (adj)	in a series

Adam Rosen's favorite *cereal* is oatmeal.
You must supply us with your *serial* number.

choose (v)	to select
chose (v)	past tense of *choose*
chews (v)	masticates, grinds with teeth

The committee must *choose* a chairperson no later
    than tomorrow.
The accused *chose* to remain silent.
She *chews* gum, and it is not very flattering.

chord (n)	a pleasant combination of tones
cord (n)	string or rope, measurement of wood

The boy could play only one *chord* on his guitar.
The *cord* of wood could not be tied with *cord*.

cite (v)	to summon or make reference to
sight (n)	that which is seen, act of seeing
site (n)	location

You must *cite* an example to prove your point.
The man caught *sight* of the blue car as it went by.
The *site* for our new building has not been determined.

clothes (n)	wearing apparel
cloths (n)	fabrics
close (v)	to terminate
(n)	the end

The *clothes* went on sale after the holiday.
The *cloths* were all imported.
We must *close* the deal by Monday morning.
She left at the *close* of the meeting.

| coarse (adj) | rough, common |
| course (n) | direction, action, part of a meal, series of studies |

My hands were *coarse* from all the washing.
Soup is served before the main *course*.
Only you can decide on the proper *course* of study.

| coma (n) | prolonged unconsciousness |
| comma (n) | mark of punctuation |

The woman was in a *coma* following the accident.
It is important to understand the uses of the *comma*.

command (n)	an order, direction, authority
(v)	to order, direct
commend (v)	to praise, to entrust

The director took full *command* of the situation.
His presence *commanded* attention.
I must *commend* you on an outstanding performance.

commence (v)	to begin
comments (n)	remarks
(v)	to make remarks

The meeting will *commence* after lunch.
His *comments* were not called for.
She *comments* after everything I say.

complement (n)	that which completes
(v)	to complete, go well with
compliment (n)	expression of praise
(v)	to express praise

A full *complement* of soldiers arrived.
That color will *complement* your room.
Your *compliment* was most appreciated.
I will *compliment* the student on her outstanding work.

confidant (n)	trusted friend or adviser (*confidante* for female)
confident (n)	sure, certain

Eric's *confidante* is Carole Sheridan.
I am *confident* that you will be successful.

conscience (n)	the sense of right and wrong
conscious (adj)	aware, having feeling

After the confession, his *conscience* was clear.
Are you *conscious* of your actions?

continual (adj)	occurring steadily or recurring frequently
continuous (adj)	happening without interruption

The bells ring every hour on a *continual* basis.
The *continuous* noise made him very nervous.

cooperation (n)	joint effort
corporation (n)	a form of business organization

Your *cooperation* will be greatly appreciated.
The *corporation* is moving its headquarters to Main
   Street.

correspondence (n)	letters
correspondents (n)	those who write

Your *correspondence* reached me this morning.
The *correspondents* had a brief meeting yesterday.

costume (n)	style of clothing
custom (n)	usual practice or habit

Her *costume* was very appropriate.
It is a *custom* for people to greet each other properly.

council (n)	an assembly
counsel (n)	an attorney, advice
(v)	to advise
consul (n)	a foreign representative

The Town *Council* will have a brief meeting this evening.

The plaintiff's *counsel* made a moving plea.
The teacher will *counsel* any student who asks.
The *consul* was granted diplomatic immunity.

credible (adj)	believable, reliable
creditable (adj)	deserving of credit
credulous (adj)	too easily convinced

She is a *credible* witness.
The soldier's bravery was *creditable*.
The lying witness convinced the *credulous* jury.

currant (n)	small fruit, berry
current (adj)	belonging to the present

They purchased a jar of *currant* jelly.
Is this the *current* issue of the magazine?

decease (v)	to die
disease (n)	an illness

Mr. Murphy has been *deceased* since 1970.
Unfortunately, his *disease* was not curable.

decent (adj)	proper, reasonably good
descent (n)	a going down, decline
dissent (n)	disagreement

He seems to be a *decent* fellow.
The *descent* from the mountain was tiring.
The problem caused much *dissent* among the normally united group.

decree (n)	official order or decision
degree (n)	successive step, measured amount

The *decree* seemed to be reasonable.
There are different *degrees* of efficiency.

defer (v)	to put off
differ (v)	to disagree

We will *defer* your payment for only one month.
The two men *differ* in their opinions.

deference (n)	a yielding of opinion, regard for another's wishes
difference (n)	dissimilarity

In *deference* to the dignitary, I will not press the issue.
There seems to be a slight *difference* of opinion.

depraved	past participle of *deprave*, morally corrupted
deprived	past participle of *deprive*, underprivileged, forced to do without

The *depraved* witness ranted and raved.
You will not be *deprived* of any necessities.

deserts (n)	deserved award or punishment
desert (n)	barren region
(v)	forsake, leave
dessert (n)	last course of a meal

The scofflaw received his just *deserts* when his car was
impounded.
The oasis in the *desert* was actually a mirage.
It is terrible to *desert* one's child.
For *dessert*, we ordered apple pie.

device (n)   plan, scheme, contrivance
devise (v)   to contrive, plan

> A new mechanical *device* will be necessary to start the machine.
> She *devised* a plan of action that should work.

disapprove (v)   to consider wrong
disprove (v)   to prove the falsity of

> I *disapprove* of immoral actions.
> The attorney tried to *disprove* the statement of the witness.

disburse (v)   to pay out, expend
disperse (v)   to break up, scatter

> I *disbursed* $25 on your behalf.
> The mob *dispersed* when the police arrived.

do (v)   to perform
due (adj)   owing or scheduled to arrive
dew (n)   moisture

> You cannot leave until you *do* your chores.
> My mortgage payment is *due* on the tenth of each month.
> The *dew* settled on the ground.

done   past participle of *do*, completed
dun (v)   demand payment

> I have *done* all my chores.
> Pay your bills, and we will not have to *dun* you.

dose (n)   extent of treatment, measured quantity

doze (v)   to nap

Take a small *dose* of the medicine.
The man *dozed* off for a few hours.

dual (adj)   double
duel (n)   a formal fight, combat

The knife has a *dual* edge.
Hamilton was killed in a *duel.*

dying   present participle of *die*
dyeing   present participle of *dye*, to color

The poor man is *dying* of cancer.
I am *dyeing* my dress red.

elicit (v)   to draw out, extract
illicit (adj)   unlawful

The candidate was trying to *elicit* money for the campaign.
They were having an *illicit* love affair.

eligible (adj)   qualified, fit to be chosen
illegible (adj)   difficult to read

The winner will be *eligible* for the $1 million drawing.
If your handwriting is *illegible*, you should consider typing.

emerge (v)   to rise from
immerge (v)   to plunge into, immerse

He *emerged* a winner.
The technician *immerged* the x-ray in a chemical bath.

| emigrate (v) | to leave or move away from |
| immigrate (v) | to move to |

The refugees *emigrated* from Russia.
They *immigrated* to America.

eminent (adj)	well-known, distinguished
imminent (adj)	threatening, impending
emanate (v)	to issue from, be emitted

He is an *eminent* politician.
I do not feel that there is any *imminent* danger.
A foul odor *emanated* from the kitchen.

ensure (v)	to make certain
insure (v)	protect against loss
assure (v)	to give confidence

I want to *ensure* your safety.
You should *insure* the package for $50.
Let me *assure* you, you are in no danger.

| envelop (v) | to wrap, surround, conceal |
| envelope (n) | a wrapper for a letter |

The members fled when smoke *enveloped* the room.
Do not forget to put your return address on the *envelope*.

| everyday (adj) | daily (used before a noun) |
| every day | each day |

Brushing your teeth should be an *everyday* activity.
For *every day* that you are late, there will be a penalty.

| everyone (n) | each one |
| every one | each one (when followed by *of*) |

Everyone will be ready at eight.
Every one of them will be ready at eight.

| expend (v) | to spend, use up |
| expand (v) | to increase in size |

They *expended* all their resources on buying a home.
They *expanded* the home by adding a den.

| expansive (adj) | widely extended |
| expensive (adj) | costly, high priced |

The *expansive* bridge joined the two cities.
Expensive does not always mean better.

fair (n)	festival, market, carnival
(adj)	according to the rules, light in color
fare (n)	money paid for transportation

I won this stuffed animal at the *fair*.
I appeal to your sense of *fair* play.
Fair skin sunburns easily.
The *fare* has gone up to 50 cents.

| farther (adj) | more distant |
| further (adv) | to a greater degree |

The drive from the airport was *farther* than we had
   expected.
We can discuss the proposal *further* at a later date.

| faze (v) | to disturb, embarrass |
| phase (n) | stage of development |

The incident did not seem to *faze* her.
We are now in the second *phase* of the project.

feat (n)	remarkable accomplishment
feet (n)	plural of *foot*

That was quite a *feat*!
My *feet* hurt after the mile hike.

finale (n)	conclusion
finally (adv)	in conclusion
finely (adv)	in a fine manner, minutely

The grand *finale* was beautiful.
He *finally* remembered to call.
She *finely* and tactfully handled the situation.

fineness (n)	delicacy
finesse (n)	ability to handle delicate situations, tact

The *fineness* of the embroidery impressed everyone.
You handled the situation with great *finesse*.

fir (n)	evergreen tree
fur (n)	pelt of an animal

Fir trees are beautiful when they are snow covered.
She received an expensive *fur* coat for her birthday.

fiscal (adj)	financial, pertaining to public revenues
physical (adj)	pertaining to the body

The *fiscal* period begins in July.
It is wise to have a *physical* examination regularly.

flair (n)   natural aptitude
flare (n)   a light or signal

She has a *flair* for design.
The *flare* warned them of impending danger.

flew (v)   past tense of *fly*, soared through the air
flu (n)   short for *influenza*
flue (n)   part of a chimney

The airplane *flew* at a very high altitude.
He was very weak after recovering from the *flu*.
You must clean your *flue* if you want to avoid a chimney fire.

flour (n)   finely chopped grain
flower (n)   blossoming plant

She used five pounds of *flour* to bake the bread.
He sent her *flowers* as a sign of love.

for (prep)   in favor of, in place of
fore (n)   front part of something
four (adj)   numeral

I will go *for* you if you are unable to attend.
In order to present the facts, he brought the witness to the *fore*.
I tried at least *four* times.

formally (adv)   in a formal manner
formerly (adv)   at an earlier time

They all dressed *formally* for the dance.
I believe that we were *formerly* classmates.

fort (n)	enclosed place of defense
forte (n)	strong point

The *fort* afforded them adequate protection.
Mathematics is not my *forte!*

forth (adv)	forward, out
fourth (n)	following third

Go *forth* and make an attempt.
On his *fourth* attempt, he crossed the hurdle.

forward (adv)	ahead, toward the front
foreword (n)	preface in a book

"*Forward*, march," yelled the captain.
The *foreword* offered valuable information about the
    author.

grate (n)	part of a fireplace
(v)	to irritate
great (adj)	large quantity, wonderful

The *grate* was covered with ashes.
The noise *grates* on my nerves.
You did a *great* job.

guessed (v)	past tense of *guess*, estimated
guest (n)	visitor

You *guessed* correctly.
Our *guest* arrived later than we had expected.

hall (n)	large room
haul (v)	to pull with force

The *hall* was beautifully decorated for the party.
I am tired; I cannot *haul* any more wood.

handsome (adj)	good-looking
hansom (n)	two-wheeled covered carriage

Richard Moeller is a *handsome* young man.
The *hansom* cab ride through Central Park was romantic.

heal (v)	to cure
heel (n)	back of the foot

Unfortunately, doctors cannot *heal* all their patients.
She had difficulty getting her *heel* into the boot.

hear (v)	to perceive by ear
here (adv)	in this place

I did not *hear* you when you called.
They are all *here*; we can start.

heard (v)	past tense of *hear*, sensed sounds
herd (n)	a group of animals

I *heard* the thunder last night and was frightened.
The *herd* of cattle trampled the rancher's land.

higher (adj)	comparative degree of high
hire (v)	to engage or employ

I scored ten points *higher* this time.
My services are not for *hire*.

holey (adj)	full of holes
wholly (adv)	completely
holly (n)	a shrub

That *holey* blouse should be thrown out.
I am *wholly* satisfied with the results.
The *holly* tree needs water.

human (n)	a person
humane (adj)	civilized, kindly

Every *human* should be free to make choices.
That was the only *humane* thing that could be done.

ideal (adj)	perfect
idle (adj)	unemployed, not working
idol (n)	object of worship

Michael Kaminsky is the *ideal* candidate for the job.
Idle machines are not productive.
Elvis Presley had always been my *idol*.

incite (v)	to stir to action
insight (n)	clear understanding

The speaker *incited* a riot by his remarks.
Eric Laurence has remarkable *insight* for one so young.

instance (n)	example, case, illustration
instants (n)	particular moments

In this *instance*, I must agree.
Our lives are mere *instants* in time.

intestate (adj)	having made no will
interstate (adj)	between states
intrastate (adj)	within a state

The man died *intestate*.
Interstate travel between New York and New Jersey

was hampered by the weather.
The New York State Thruway is an *intrastate* highway.

its (pron)	belonging to it
it's (contraction)	it is

The company fired *its* president.
It's too late to go to a restaurant.

knew (v)	past tense of *know*, perceived
new (adj)	not old

The chairman *knew* of the incident.
The *new* building attracted many visitors.

know (v)	to understand, perceive
no (adj)	not any

I *know* of a good electrician.
There is *no* chance of getting the appointment.

lapse (v)	to become void
elapse (v)	to pass
relapse (v)	to slip back into a former condition

The policy will *lapse* if it is not paid by the tenth of
    the month.
If you let too much time *elapse*, we will not reinstate
    the policy.
He regained consciousness and then *relapsed* into a
    coma.

later (adv)	more recent, after a time
latter (adj)	second in a series of two

I will return the book *later*.
Of Tom and Marc, the *latter* should qualify.

lay (v)	to place an object down
lie (v)	to recline
(n)	an untruth

Please *lay* the package down at the front door.
I would like to *lie* down for a while.
He told a *lie*, and he was punished.

lead (n)	a heavy metal
(v)	to guide
led (v)	past tense of *lead*, guided

The *lead* pipe was too heavy to lift.
The majorette will *lead* the parade.
The majorette *led* the parade.

lean (v)	to bend or incline
(adj)	thin, not fat or fatty
lien (n)	claim against property as security for a debt

If you *lean* against the post, it might fall.
That is a juicy, *lean* piece of steak.
The judge ordered a *lien* against Mr. Smith's salary.

leased (v)	past tense of *lease*, rented or contracted
least (n)	smallest in size

They *leased* the property for one year.
That is the *least* important thing on my mind.

legislator (n)	member of a lawmaking body
legislature (n)	lawmaking body

Each *legislator* is entitled to one vote.
The *legislature* voted in favor of the bill.

lessen (v)	to make less, decrease
lesson (n)	something that is to be learned, instruction

That will certainly *lessen* your chances for the position.

Take a *lesson* from what happened.

levee (n)	bank along a river
levy (v)	to impose a tax

The *levee* was dry due to the drought.

The government may *levy* additional taxes to balance the budget.

liable (adj)	legally bound, responsible
libel (n)	false written statements

You are *liable* for your promise.

Mrs. Jones is being sued for *libel*.

lightening (v)	making lighter
lightning (n)	atmospheric electricity

By *lightening* her burden, we helped her cross the street.

Jonathan was awakened by the thunder and *lightning*.

local (adj)	confined to a certain place
locale (n)	a particular place, setting for a story

That is a *local* issue; do not interfere.

I believe the *locale* was Virginia.

loose (v)	to set free
lose (v)	to suffer a loss, mislay
loss (n)	something lost

They set the animals *loose*.
Leave early, in case you *lose* your way.
He could not be compensated for the severe *loss* of property.

mail (n)	correspondence
male (n)	masculine person

The *mail* piled up while I was on vacation.
Every eighteen-year-old *male* must register for the draft.

manner (n)	a way of acting, procedure
manor (n)	estate

In what *manner* do you wish to proceed?
The *manor* stood amid the graceful willow trees.

marital (adj)	pertaining to marriage
martial (adj)	pertaining to the military
marshal (n)	an official

Marv and Barbara are having *marital* problems.
Martial law has been declared.
A new *marshal* will be chosen in two months.

maybe (adv)	perhaps
may be (v)	might be

If we don't receive his letter, *maybe* we should call.
Mr. Karp *may be* out of town tomorrow.

meat (n)	flesh of animals
meet (n)	an assembly or race
(v)	to come together
mete (v)	to measure, distribute

I like my *meat* rare.
The track *meet* was canceled because of the weather.
We will *meet* tomorrow for lunch.
The judge had to *mete* out the sentence based on the decision of the jury.

medal (n)	badge of honor
meddle (v)	to interfere
metal (n)	kind of element or alloy
mettle (n)	high quality, courage, spirit

For his bravery, he received a *medal*.
Do not *meddle* in the lives of others.
Gold is a very expensive *metal*.
Fran proved her *mettle* by her courageous act.

miner (n)	one who works in a mine
minor (n)	person under legal age

The California gold rush brought many *miners* to the West.
A *minor* cannot be sold alcoholic beverages.

mist (n)	haze, light fog
missed (v)	past tense of *miss*, failed to do

The *mist* was so thick we could not see the Golden Gate Bridge.
We *missed* you at the meeting yesterday.

moral (n)	lesson relating to right and wrong
morale (n)	spirit or mental condition

Many a story has a *moral*.
Morale was very low after we heard the bad news.

morning (n)	time before noon
mourning (v)	expressing grief

The *morning* air is so clean and fresh.
The man is *mourning* the death of his wife.

motif (n)	theme
motive (n)	intention or inner drive

The *motif* for the party will be the fifties.
We cannot determine a *motive* in this case.

none (pron)	not one, not any
no one (pron)	nobody

None of the packages were properly wrapped.
No one in the group had any objections.

ophthalmologist (n)	a doctor who treats eyes
optician (n)	one who makes or sells eyeglasses
optometrist (n)	one who measures vision

Very delicate eye surgery was performed by the
   ophthalmologist.
The *optician* recommended oval frames.
The *optometrist* determined his vision to be 20/20.

one (adj)	numeral
won (v)	past tense of *win*, triumphed

One more chance is all you will have.
The Yankees have *won* the World Series more times
   than any other team.

overdo (v)	to do in excess
overdue (adj)	past due or late

It is unwise to *overdo* exercises when you are not in good shape.

Your *overdue* account will result in late charges.

packed	past participle of *pack*, bundled, pressed together
pact (n)	an agreement

The vase was *packed* in paper to avoid breakage.

The *pact* we made is binding on both of us.

pain (n)	suffering or strong discomfort
pane (n)	window glass

The patient experienced a great deal of *pain* after the operation.

The window *pane* must be replaced before winter.

pair (n)	two similar things
pare (v)	to reduce or peel
pear (n)	a fruit

The *pair* of shoes you like is now on sale.

You must *pare* an orange before you eat it.

I took the juicy, green *pear* from the fruit bowl.

parameter (n)	assigned value, reference for determining values
perimeter (n)	outer boundary or area

Certain *parameters* have been set, and we must abide by them.

The *perimeter* is larger than we had originally estimated.

partition (n)	division
petition (n)	formal request

The *partition* has afforded the two secretaries much
more privacy.

A *petition* is being circulated among the students.

passed (v)	past tense of *pass*, moved along, trans-ferred, lead
past (n)	history, time gone by

I *passed* your house on the way home from work.

I will not reveal anything about your *past*.

patience (n)	endurance, composure
patients (n)	persons receiving treatment

My *patience* is wearing thin.

Dr. Zisman has many *patients* in the waiting room.

peace (n)	state of calm, freedom from war
piece (n)	portion or fragment

We all wish for *peace* throughout the world.

A *piece* of the pie is missing.

peak (n)	top
peek (n)	glance

The view from the *peak* of the mountain was breath-taking.

Do not *peek* around the corner.

peal (n)	ringing of a bell
peel (v)	to strip off

The *peal* of the church bells echoed through the hills.

Many people will *peel* an apple before eating it.

pedal (n)	foot-operated lever
peddle (v)	to sell
petal (n)	part of a flower

Do not step so hard on the gas *pedal*!
You are not allowed to *peddle* your wares on this corner.
Each rose *petal* glistened from the dew.

peer (n)	equal in rank
pier (n)	a wharf or dock

You will be judged by a jury of your *peers*.
We could not see the *pier* due to the heavy fog.

perfect (adj)	flawless
(v)	to bring to completion
prefect (n)	an official

She is a *perfect* example of brains and beauty.
The writer must *perfect* the story before publication.
The *prefect* doled out the necessary punishment.

persecute (v)	to oppress, harass, annoy
prosecute (v)	to institute legal proceedings against

Many people throughout the world are *persecuted*.
The criminal was *prosecuted* for embezzlement.

personal (adj)	private
personnel (n)	staff, workers

The quarrel was brought about by a *personal* matter.
All *personnel* will be required to attend the meeting.

perspective (n)	appearance, point of view
prospective (adj)	anticipated, apt

When things look bad, you must keep your *perspective*.
The Greens have a *prospective* buyer for their home.

peruse (v)	to study or read
pursue (v)	to chase, follow, overtake

Peruse the contract carefully before signing.
The police had to *pursue* the suspect for an hour.

physic (n)	laxative
physique (n)	bodily structure
psychic (adj)	pertaining to mind or spirit

A *physic* will help to cleanse your system.
Exercising will help a person's *physique*.
A man with *psychic* powers was called in to help find
the missing child.

plain (n)	flat field
(adj)	clear, obvious
plane (n)	tool to make level

Many pioneers perished attempting to cross the *plains*.
The *plain* truth is sometimes difficult to accept.
The carpenter used a new *plane* to smooth the surface.

plaintiff (n)	party instituting a lawsuit
plaintive (adj)	mournful

The *plaintiff* will call her first witness.
The *plaintive* cry of the wolf sent chills down my spine.

pleas (n)	appeals, statements, allegations
please (v)	to be agreeable

The attorney will enter two guilty *pleas*.
You cannot *please* everyone!

pole (n)	long, slender piece of metal or wood
poll (n)	counting, voting place, registering of persons
(v)	to count, canvass

The telephone *pole* toppled from the weight of the ice.

The *polls* will open at nine.

The students were *polled* for their opinions.

precede (v)	to go before
proceed (v)	to advance
procedure (n)	method (note the single *e*)

"A" *precedes* "B" in the alphabet.

The directions state: "*Proceed* to the second traffic light."

Filing this form is standard *procedure* for requesting a loan.

preposition (n)	part of speech
proposition (n)	offer or appeal

"Of" is a *preposition*.

Your *proposition* is too good to refuse.

presence (n)	existence, attendance
presents (n)	gifts
(v)	introduces formally

Your *presence* is required at a minimum of ten meetings.

Buy your Christmas *presents* early, and avoid the rush.

The emcee formally *presents* all of the guest speakers.

principal (n)	sum of money, school official
(adj)	main, first in rank, leading
principle (n)	rule, value

The loan, including *principal* and interest, amounted to $321.

The company's *principal* headquarters will be on Main Street.

A candidate should be a person of *principle*.

profit (n)	monetary gain
prophet (n)	one who forecasts future events

All the partners should show a *profit* from the merger.

The *prophet* foretold the events.

propose (v)	offer, suggest
purpose (n)	intention

I would like to *propose* a toast.

The *purpose* of our visit should be obvious.

quiet (n)	stillness
quite (adv)	considerably, completely
quit (v)	to stop, abandon

The *quiet* of the country was a pleasant change from the noisy city.

I am *quite* certain that I am correct.

Do not *quit* your job until you have found another.

rain (n)	precipitation
rein (n)	harness
reign (n)	term of a ruler's power

The *rain* helped to fill the thirsty reservoirs.
Adam held the *reins* with all his might.
A *reign* of terror prevailed under his dictatorship.

raise (v)	to lift, elevate
rays (n)	beams
raze (v)	to demolish or destroy

Raise your glass, and toast the new year.
The *rays* of the sun shone brightly on the newly fallen
   snow.
Construction crews will *raze* many of the old build-
   ings.

rap (v)	to knock
wrap (n)	outer grament
(v)	to enclose

Rap twice, and I will know it is you.
You may need a warmer *wrap* this chilly evening.
Wrap the package securely.

| rapt (adj) | engrossed, absorbed |
| wrapped (v) | past tense of *wrap* |

Sheryl was held in *rapt* silence by the movie.
The meat was *wrapped* in aluminum foil.

read (v)	to perform the act of reading
reed (n)	a plant, musical instrument
red (adj)	a color

If one *reads*, one can learn a lot.
The *reeds* swayed with the breeze.
If you mix *red* and yellow, you get orange.

| reality (n) | actuality |
| realty (n) | real estate |

The *reality* of the situation did not hit us until later.
The *realty* office will close for the holiday.

| recent (adj) | of the near past |
| resent (v) | to be indignant about |

I saw your article in a *recent* issue of the magazine.
I *resent* that accusation!

| reference (n) | that which refers to something |
| reverence (n) | deep respect |

You will find the information in *reference* books.
His *reverence* for money created problems between
   friends.

| residence (n) | dwelling, house |
| residents (n) | people who reside |

This enormous *residence* should sell for over $100,000.
The *residents* of this home will be away for two weeks.

| respectfully (adv) | in a respectful manner |
| respectively (adv) | in the order listed |

The letter was signed, "*Respectfully* yours."
I gave the pail and shovel to Jack and Sandy respec-
   tively.

right (adj)	correct
(n)	just privilege
rite (n)	formal ceremony
write (v)	to inscribe

All the answers were *right* for a grade of 100 percent.
You have the *right* to sue.
Last *rites* were administered to the accident victim.
Please *write*, and let me know the answer.

role (n)	part in a play, function
roll (n)	register or list, small bread

This *role* will give her the opportunity to sing and
  dance.
The *roll* shows that you were absent twice last se-
  mester.

root (n)	part of a plant
route (n)	an established course of travel

Roots must receive water for the plant to grow.
You will find the shortest *route* by checking the map.

rote (n)	routine, repetition
wrote (v)	past tense of *write*

Marc learned his spelling words by *rote*.
I *wrote* a letter to you yesterday.

sail (n)	canvas part of a boat
(v)	to travel by water by means of sails
sale (n)	the act of selling, a selling at reduced prices

We had to replace the *sail* because of a large hole.
I would love to *sail* to Bermuda.
The store is crowded when it is running a *sale*.

scene (n)	a setting, place where something oc-curs
seen	past participle of *see*, observed

You could not have picked a prettier *scene* for the
    painting.
I had *seen* the accident on my way home.

| seam (n) | line of junction |
| seen (v) | to appear |

seam (n)   line of junction
seem (v)   to appear

The *seam* on her dress was opening.
Things are not always what they *seem* to be.

sell (v)   trade or transfer for a price
cell (n)   a small compartment

Do not *sell* the stock until the price increases.
The prisoner was confined to his *cell* as a punishment.

seller (n)   one who sells
cellar (n)   level below ground

The *seller* dictated all the terms of the agreement.
Our *cellar* flooded during the heavy rain storm.

sew (v)   to stitch
so (adv)   in such manner, thus
sow (v)   to scatter seed

Denise must *sew* the dress if she is to wear it tomorrow.
I will stay home *so* that you will be able to attend.
If you *sow* seeds in the spring, you can harvest them
    in the fall.

simple (adj)   not difficult
simplistic (adj) oversimplified

This problem is *simple*.
You are sheltering yourself by taking such a *simplistic*
    viewpoint.

soared (v)	past tense of *soar*, flew
sword (n)	weapon

The airplane *soared* to great heights.
The *sword* pierced his skin during the duel.

some (adj)	part of
sum (n)	amount, total

Some of you will have to stay behind.
You owe me a large *sum* of money.

son (n)	male child
sun (n)	source of light

Marc Alan is my first-born *son*.
The *sun* disappeared behind the clouds.

stair (n)	a step
stare (v)	to look at

The rug on that *stair* should be replaced.
It is uncomfortable to have someone *stare* at you.

stake (n)	a pointed stick, prize in a contest
steak (n)	slice of meat or fish

Mr. Lorenz has a large *stake* in the outcome of this project.
The *steak* sizzled on the greasy grill.

stationary (adj)	fixed, not moving
stationery (n)	writing paper

Old schoolhouses had *stationary* desks and chairs.
Please order buff *stationery* and matching envelopes.

statue (n)	a carved or molded figure
stature (n)	height of a person
statute (n)	law or regulation

The *Statue* of Liberty has welcomed many foreigners.
The accountant is a woman of sizeable *stature*.
What is the *statute* of limitations for armed robbery?

steal (v)	to take unlawfully
steel (n)	a form of iron

If you *steal*, you can be arrested.
The *steel* strike created heavy unemployment.

suit (n)	set of clothes
(v)	to please or make appropriate
suite (n)	set of rooms, matched pieces of furniture
sweet (adj)	having a sugary taste

A dark business *suit* will be appropriate for the interview.
That style *suits* him.
Please reserve a *suite* of rooms for the conference.
Sugar will make your coffee *sweet*.

taught (v)	past tense of *teach*, instructed
taut (adj)	tightly drawn, tense

The child will have to be *taught* a lesson.
The rope must be *taut* or the boat will drift.

team (n)	group that works together
teem (v)	to abound

We will need a *team* of experts to make that decision.
The ocean *teems* with beautiful plant and fish life.

tear (n)	water from the eyes
tier (n)	a row or layer

A single *tear* fell from the clown's eye.
Your seat is located in the top *tier* of the balcony.

tenant (n)	one who pays rent
tenet (n)	principle or belief

The *tenant* pays the landlord $450 per month.
The basic *tenet* of his argument was implausible.

than (conj)	comparison expressing exception
then (adv)	at that time, next

Gold is more expensive *than* silver.
I will go home and *then* call you.

their (pron)	belonging to them
there (adv)	in that place
they're (contrac- tion)	they are

The students will receive *their* grades tomorrow.
Please place the packages over *there*.
They're making a very worthwhile investment.

therefor (adv)	for this, for it
therefore (adv)	consequently, as a result

I paid $1,000 for the car but received $1,500 *therefor*.
You will, *therefore*, have to surrender the merchandise.

threw (v)	past tense of *throw*
through (prep)	from one end to another, by means of
thorough (adj)	carried through to completion

Reggie Jackson *threw* the ball, and the runner was out.

If you look *through* the eyehole of a kaleidoscope, you will see a beautiful pattern.

They made a *thorough* investigation of the evidence.

to (prep)	toward, in the direction of
too (adv)	also, more than enough, excessive
two (adj)	numeral

We walked *to* the park.
He ate *too* much for dinner.
Eric has *two* rabbits, Bunny and Cinnamon.

trial (n)	examination, hardship
trail (n)	path

The defendant's *trial* is scheduled for March 20.
The rabbit left a *trail* in the newly fallen snow.

trustee (n)	one to whom something is entrusted
trusty (adj)	dependable

Raye appointed her nephew as *trustee* for her estate.
Her nephew is a *trusty*, hard-working young man.

undo (v)	to open, render ineffective
undue (adj)	improper, excessive

The man could not *undo* the harm that he had caused.
The attorney placed the witness under *undue* pressure.

urban (adj)	pertaining to the city
urbane (adj)	polished, suave

Urban living has many advantages.
The *urbane* gentleman charmed women with his wit.

vain (adj)	proud, conceited
vane (n)	device for measuring wind, weather-cock
vein (n)	blood vessel, bed of mineral materials

The woman went on a diet because she was *vain* about her appearance.

The weather *vane* spun furiously in the high wind.

His doctor thought the *vein* might be blocked by a blood clot.

vendee (n)	purchaser
vendor (n)	seller

The *vendee* paid $1 million for the purchase of the property.

The *vendor* received $1 million for the sale of the property.

vice- (adj)	prefix for designated titles of office
vice (n)	moral failing
vise (n)	a clamp

She was appointed *vice-president* in charge of sales.

Smoking and alcohol are two of his many *vices*.

The *vise* held the wood in place.

waist (n)	middle part of the body
waste (n)	needless destruction or expenditure
(v)	to expend needlessly

The belt fit snugly around her *waist*.

The *waste* of time was completely unnecessary.

If you *waste* money, you will have none left when needed.

wait (v)   to stay, remain
weight (n)   heaviness

> I have to *wait* for my friend.
> His excessive *weight* made it difficult to buy clothes.

waive (v)   to forego, relinquish
wave (n)   gesture, surge of water

> The bank will *waive* all penalties.
> The crested *wave* broke against the sandy, white beach.

wares (n)   goods for sale
wear (v)   to have on, carry on your person
were (v)   form of *to be*
where (adv)   in, at, at the place

> The vendor sold his *wares* on the busy corner.
> The bride will *wear* a satin gown to her wedding.
> *Where* *were* you last night?

way (n)   direction, distance, manner
weigh (v)   to find the weight of

> Which *way* to San Francisco?
> It is best to *weigh* yourself in the morning.

weak (adj)   lacking strength
week (n)   period of seven days

> You are too *weak* to lift the piece of furniture.
> We will meet for lunch on Wednesday of next *week*.

weather (n)   condition of the atmosphere
       (v)   to come through safely
whether (conj)   if, in case

We cannot do much about the *weather*.
If properly dressed, you will *weather* the storm.
Find out *whether* this contract is acceptable.

who's (contraction)	who is, who has
whose (pron)	possessive of *who*, belonging to whom

"*Who's* there?" the woman called.
Please tell me *whose* paper this is.

woman (n)	female person
women (n)	female people

The *woman* left her coat at the restaurant.
The *women* left their coats at the restaurant.

your (pron)	belonging to you
you're (contraction)	you are

Please make sure to gather *your* belongings before
    leaving.
You're a very lucky person.

CHAPTER 9

ABBREVIATIONS

Academic Degrees, Acronyms, Broadcasting Systems, Companies and Organizations, Compass Points, Geographical Terms, Government Agencies, Measurements, Titles, Commonly Used Abbreviations

The abbreviation serves as a space-saving device and is widely used in tables, footnotes, invoices, and so forth. Careful writers, however, avoid using abbreviations in the body of most written material. The rule of thumb among writers is, "If in doubt, write it out."

When using abbreviations, you must be certain that the intended reader will understand your reference. When you hear or see *CIA*, for example, you undoubtedly think of the Central Intelligence Agency. Are you aware that the Culinary Institute of America bears the same initials? Confusion can be avoided by writing out your intended reference followed by the abbreviation in parentheses.

A recent report published by the American Bar Association (ABA). . . . The ABA further reports . . .

Leading authorities cannot agree on the capitalization or punctuation of many abbreviations; therefore, it is wise to check a dictionary and to be consistent within the same written material.

Abbreviations that have no periods are typed with no space between the letters; abbreviations that have periods are typed with no spaces after the inside periods and one at the conclusion of the abbreviation. (The exception to this latter rule is personal names: H. G. Wells.)

The following guidelines should be of value.

Academic Degrees

Academic degrees that appear at the end of a name are abbreviated, using capital letters with a period after each part.

> Susan Bergstein, R.N.
> Marvin Karp, Ph.D.
> Janice Teisch, M.A.

Acronyms

An acronym is a word that derives from its initial letters. *NATO* (North American Treaty Organization) is an acronym whereas *FBI* (Federal Bureau of Investigation) is not. In the latter, you say each letter and do not use the initials as a word. Most acronyms are commonly used abbreviations and are easily recognizable. Each letter is placed in capital letters and periods are avoided.

> CORE (Congress of Racial Equality)
> NOW (National Organization of Women)

OPEC (Organization of Petroleum-Exporting Countries)
ZIP (Zone Improvement Plan)

Broadcasting Systems

All television and radio stations are written in capital letters with no periods.

ABC (American Broadcasting Company)
CBS (Columbia Broadcasting System)
Station WQXR-FM

Companies and Organizations

When uncertain whether a company writes out or abbreviates parts of its name, check the letterhead or a telephone book, if available. *Inc.* and *Ltd.* are commonly abbreviated; the ampersand (&) can be either the symbol or word *and*. If in doubt, write it out.

Many well-known business firms, unions, agencies, and so forth commonly abbreviate their names. These abbreviations are usually written without periods.

AT&T (American Telephone & Telegraph Company)
FCC (Federal Communications Commission)
IBM (International Business Machines)
YMCA (Young Men's Christian Association)

Compass Points

Compass points are generally written out unless they follow a street address or designate a section of a city.

356 Washington Avenue, N.E.
124 East Fifth Avenue

Geographical Terms

Names of countries, cities, and states should usually be written out. Exceptions include:

1. U.S.A., U.S.S.R., U.A.R. (periods inserted)
2. Two-letter state abbreviations on envelopes and inside addresses. (no periods used) A list of such abbreviations can be found in the "Postal Services" chapter.
3. *St.* Louis, but *Fort* Lauderdale. If in doubt about others, check a dictionary.

Government Agencies

Well-known agencies (national and international) are often abbreviated with all capital letters and no periods.

FDA (Food and Drug Administration)
HEW (Department of Health, Education, and Welfare)
IRS (Internal Revenue Service)
UN (United Nations)

Measurements

Units of measure (weights, distances, etc.) should not be abbreviated except in technical writings, tables, and some business forms, with the exception of temperature measures.

> The 50-gallon container rolled off the truck.
> The weatherman reported a delightful 75°F for tomorrow.

Titles

Personal titles that appear before and after names are generally abbreviated. You capitalize the first letter and place a period after the final letter.

> Mrs. Elaine Nicolucci
> Hon. Ethel Lorenz
> Carl Wanderman, Esq. (attorney)
> Dr. Howard Rosen

Commonly Used Abbreviations

A.A.	Associate of Arts (degree)
AAA	American Automobile Association
ABA	American Bar Association, American Bankers Association

abbr.	abbreviation
a/c or acct.	account
ACLU	American Civil Liberties Union
A.D.	(*anno Domini*) after the birth of Christ
addl.	additional
ad val. or A/V	(*ad valorum*) according to value
AFL-CIO	American Federation of Labor and Congress of Industrial Organizations
AIDS	Acquired Immune Deficiency Syndrome
a.k.a. or a/k/a	also known as
a.m. (AM)	(*ante meridiem*) before noon
AMA	American Medical Association American Management Association
AMEX	American Stock Exchange
amt.	amount
anon.	anonymous
a/o	(on) account of
app.	appendix
ARC	American Red Cross
ARMA	Association of Record Managers and Administrators
ASAP	as soon as possible
ASPCA	American Society for the Prevention of Cruelty to Animals
ASTA	American Society of Travel Agents, Inc.
att.	attached
atty.	attorney
A/V	audiovisual
Ave.	Avenue
avg.	average
AWOL	absent without leave (military term)
B.A.	Bachelor of Arts (degree)

bal.	balance
BBB	Better Business Bureau
BBC	British Broadcasting Corporation
bbl.	barrel
B.C.	before Christ
B/L	bill of lading
bldg.	building
Blvd.	Boulevard
Bro.	Brother; Bros., Brothers
B/S	bill of sale
B.S.	Bachelor of Science (degree)
Btu	British thermal unit
bu.	bulletin, bureau, bushel(s)
bx	box
C	Celsius, hundred, or Congress
c. or ca.	(*circa*) approximately
CARE	Cooperative for American Relief to Everywhere
CB	Citizens' Band (radio)
cc	carbon copy (copies), cubic centimeter(s)
CD	Certificate of Deposit
CDC	Centers for Disease Control
CEO	Chief Executive Officer
CFO	Chief Financial Officer
cg.	centigram(s)
ch.	chapter
chg.	charge
CIA	Central Intelligence Agency
c.i.f. or CIF	cost, insurance, and freight
cm.	centimeter
Co.	Company
c/o	in care of
c.o.d. or COD	cash (or collect) on delivery
cont.	continued
co-op	cooperative

CORE	Congress of Racial Equality
Corp.	Corporation
CPA	Certified Public Accountant
CPO	Chief Petty Officer (military term)
CPS	Certified Professional Secretary
cr.	credit
CRT	cathode-ray tube
CST or C.S.T.	Central Standard Time
ctn.	carton
cu.	cubic
cu. cm.	cubic centimeter(s)
cu. ft.	cubic feet
DA	District Attorney
d/b/a or d.b.a.	doing business as
D.D.	Doctor of Divinity (member of clergy)
D.D.S.	Doctor of Dentistry
dept.	department
dft.	draft
dis.	discount
distr.	distributor
div.	dividend, division
DJIA	Dow Jones Industrial Average
dls/shr	dollars per share
DOA	dead on arrival
DOD	Department of Defense
DOT	Department of Transportation
doz.	dozen
DP	data processing
Dr.	doctor
dr.	debit, debtor, drawer
DST or D.S.T.	Daylight Savings Time
dstn.	destination
dtd.	dated

DX	diagnosis
D/y	delivery
E	East
ea.	each
ed.	education, editor, edition
Ed.D.	Doctor of Education (degree)
Ed.M.	Master of Education (degree)
EDT or E.D.T.	Eastern Daylight Time
EEC	European Economic Community (Common Market)
EEG	electroencephalogram
e.g.	(*exempli gratia*) for example
EKG	electrocardiogram
enc.	enclosure
end.	endorse, endorsement
EOM or e.o.m.	end of month
EP	European Plan
EPA	Environmental Protection Agency
ESL	English as a Second Language
ESP	extrasensory perception
EST or E.S.T.	Eastern Standard Time
ETA	estimated time of arrival
et al.	(*et alii*) and others
etc.	(*et cetera*) and so forth
ETD	estimated time of departure
et seq.	(*et sequens*) and the following
F or F.	Fahrenheit
FAA	Federal Aviation Administration
fac. or FAX	facsimile
FBI	Federal Bureau of Investigation
FCC	Federal Communications Commission
FDA	Food and Drug Administration
FDIC	Federal Deposit Insurance Corporation
Fed.	Federal
FHA	Federal Housing Administration

FICA	Federal Insurance Contributions Act
FIFO	first in, first out
fig.	figure
fl. oz.	fluid ounce(s)
FM	frequency modulation
fn.	footnote
FNMA	Federal National Mortgage Association (Fannie Mae)
f.o.b. or FOB	free on board
frt.	freight
FSLIC	Federal Savings and Loan Insurance Corporation
ft.	foot, feet
FTC	Federal Trade Commission
fwd.	forward
F.Y.I.	for your information
g or gr.	gram(s)
gal.	gallon(s)
GAO	General Accounting Office
GATT	General Agreement of Tariffs and Trade
GDP	Gross Domestic Product
GMAT	Graduate Management Admission Test
GNMA	Government National Mortgage Association (Ginnie Mae)
GNP	Gross National Product
GOP	Grand Old Party (Republicans)
GRE	Graduate Record Examination
gr.	gross
hdlg.	handling
hdqrs. or hq.	headquarters
Hon.	Honorable
h.p.	horsepower
hr.	hour(s)
H.R. or HR	House of Representatives
HUD	Housing and Urban Development

ibid.	(*ibidem*) the same
ICC	Interstate Commerce Commission
ICU	intensive care unit
id.	(*idem*) the same
i.e.	(*id est*) that is
ill.	illustration
IMF	International Monetary Fund
in.	inch(es)
Inc.	Incorporated
INS	Immigration and Naturalization Service
ins.	insurance
int.	interest
Int.	international
inv.	invoice
I/O	Input/Output
IOU	I owe you
IQ	intelligence quotient
IRA	Individual Retirement Account
irreg.	irregular
IRS	Internal Revenue Service
ital.	italics
IWPA	International Word Processing Association
J.D.	(*jurum doctor*) Doctor of Laws
JP	Justice of the Peace
Jr.	Junior
k.	knot
kg.	kilogram
kilo.	kilometer, kilogram
km	kilometer(s)
KO	knockout
kt.	carat
kw.	kilowatt

L	liter(s)
LASER or laser	Light amplification by stimulated emission of radiation
lat.	latitude
l., ll.	line, lines
lb.	pound(s)
LC	Library of Congress
lc	lowercase
LIFO	last in, first out
loc. cit.	(*loco citato*) in the place cited
L.S. or LS	(*locus sigilli*) place of seal for signatures
Ltd.	limited
m.	meter, married, masculine
M	Monsieur; MM, Messieurs
M	thousand
M.A.	Master of Arts (degree)
max.	maximum
M.B.A.	Master of Business Administration (degree)
MC	Master of Ceremonies, Member of Congress
M.D.	Doctor of Medicine (degree)
mdse.	merchandise
mfg.	manufacturing
mfr.	manufacturer
mg.	milligram(s)
mgr.	manager
mi.	mile(s)
min.	minute(s)
misc.	miscellaneous
Mlle.	Mademoiselle
mm.	millimeter(s)
Mme.	Madam; Mmes., Mesdames

mo.	month(s)
MO	money order
M.P.	Member of Parliament
mph or m.p.h.	miles per hour
ms.	manuscript; mss., manuscripts
MST or M.S.T.	Mountain Standard Time
msgr.	messenger
Msgr.	Monsignor
mtg.	meeting
mtge.	mortgage
mun.	municipal, municipality
N	North, net
n/30	net in 30 days
NA or N/A	not applicable
NAACP	National Association for the Advancement of Colored People
NAM	National Association of Manufacturers
NASA	National Aeronautics and Space Administration
natl.	national
NATO	North Atlantic Treaty Organization
N.B.	(*nota bene*) note well
n/c	no charge, no credit
NCCJ	National Conference of Christians and Jews
NIH	National Institutes of Health
NLRB	National Labor Relations Board
No.	number
NOAA	National Oceanic and Atmospheric Administration
NOW	National Organization for Women
NPS	National Park Service
NRA	National Rifle Association
NRC	Nuclear Regulatory Commission

NSA	National Secretaries Association
NSC	National Security Council
NSF	National Science Foundation
nt. wt.	net weight
NYSE	New York Stock Exchange
OAS	Organization of American States
OCR	optical character recognition
offic.	official
OMB	Office of Management and Budget
op. cit.	(*opere citato*) in the work cited
OPEC	Organization of Petroleum-Exporting Countries
OR	operating room
OSHA	Occupational Safety and Health Administration
oz.	ounce
p., pp.	page, pages
PAC	political action committee (plural, PAC's)
PBS	Public Broadcasting Service
pd.	paid
PDT or P.D.T.	Pacific Daylight Time
pfd.	preferred
Ph.D.	Doctor of Philosophy (degree)
PIN	personal identification number
PIRG	Public Interest Research Group
pkg.	package
p.m. or PM	(*post meridiem*) afternoon
P/N	promissory note
PO or P.O.	post office, purchase order
ppd.	postage paid in advance
PR	public relations
pro tem.	(*pro tempore*) for the time being
PS or P.S.	post script
PSAT	Preliminary Scholastic Assessment Test

PST or P.S.T.	Pacific Standard Time
pt.	pint
PTA	Parent-Teacher Association
PX	post exchange
Q	question, query
qt.	quart
qtr.	quarter
qty.	quantity
RADAR or radar	radio detection and ranging
RAM	random access memory
R&R	rest and recreation
R&D	research and development
RC	Roman Catholic
re. or ref.	reference
recd.	recorded
reg.	registered
req.	requisition
RFD	rural free delivery
rm.	ream(s), room
R.N.	registered nurse
ROTC	Reserve Officers' Training Corps
rpm	revolutions per minute
RR	railroad
RSVP	(*répondez s'il vous plaît*) please reply
rte	route
S	South
/S/ or S/	signed
S&L('s)	savings and loan(s)
SAT	Scholastic Assessment Test
SBA	Small Business Administration
sc., scil., or ss.	(*scilicet*) namely
SE	southeast
sec.	secretary, section, second

SEC	Securities and Exchange Commission
s/h	shipping/handling
SI	Système International d'Unités
sic	thus
SOP	standard operating procedure
SOS	call for help
SSA	Social Security Administration
sq. ft.	square foot
sq. in.	square inch
Sr.	Senior
SRO	standing room only
SSS	Selective Service System
St.	street
stet	let it stand (proofreading)
Supt.	superintendent
supvr.	supervisor
syn.	synonymous
TB	tuberculosis
t.b.	trial balance
TBA	to be announced
TKO	technical knockout (boxing)
TLC	tender loving care
treas.	treasurer
UAW	United Automobile Workers
u.c.	uppercase
UGT	urgent
UHF	ultrahigh frequency
UK	United Kingdom
UL	Underwriters' Laboratory
UN	United Nations
UNESCO	United Nations Educational, Scientific, and Cultural Organization
UPS	United Parcel Service

U.S.A. or USA	United States of America, United States Army
USIA	U.S. Information Agency
USMA	United States Military Academy
USN	United States Navy
USO	United Service Organizations
USPS	U.S. Postal Service
U/w	underwriter
VA	Veterans' Administration
VCR	Video Cassette Recorder
VFW	Veterans of Foreign Wars
VHF	very high frequency
VIP	very important person
viz.	(*videlicit*) namely
vol.	volume
VP	vice-president
vs. or v.	versus
W	West
WATS	Wide-Area Telephone Service
whsle.	wholesale
wk.	week(s)
w/o	without
WP	word processing
wpm	words per minute
wt.	weight
yd.	yard(s)
YMCA	Young Men's Christian Association
YMHA	Young Men's Hebrew Association
yr.	year(s)
YWCA	Young Women's Christian Association

| YWHA | Young Women's Hebrew Association |
| ZIP | Zone Improvement Plan |

Part II.
Communication
Techniques
and
Procedures

CHAPTER 10

LETTERS, MEMOS, AND POSTAL CARDS

Letter Styles, Standard Letter Parts, Two-Page Letters, Envelopes, Two-Letter State Abbreviations, Interoffice Memos, Postal Cards

We are a nation that creates paperwork—and letters and memos are the second most common type of business communication, after forms.

Whether your letter is dictated by your employer or originated by you, its organization, completeness, accuracy, clarity, and neatness are your responsibility. When your letter is typed, it should be one on which you are proud to place your signature or reference initials.

Letter Styles

Your letter should be vertically and horizontally centered so that the margins form an imaginary frame around the type-written portion. The following guidelines should assist you in determining your horizontal and vertical spacing.

a short letter (approximately 125 words or less)
vertical spacing: 19–20 lines from the top
horizontal spacing: 17–67 margins (pica)
                    25–75 margins (elite)

an average letter (approximately 126–225 words)
vertical spacing: 15–18 lines from the top
horizontal spacing: 17–67 margins (pica)
                    20–80 margins (elite)

a long letter (approximately 226 words or more)
vertical spacing: 10–12 lines from the top
horizontal spacing: 12–72 margins (pica)
                    15–85 margins (elite)

Samples of some of the most common letter styles are shown on pages 179–182.

Standard Letter Parts

(1) DATE LINE

The current date, using no abbreviations, starts on vertical line 15–18 for a standard letter. For horizontal placement, see *Letter Styles*.

September 16, 19XX

(2) MAILING OR IN-HOUSE NOTATIONS

Mailing notations (special delivery, certified mail, registered mail, air mail, by messenger) or in-house notations (personal, confidential) are placed two lines below the date either in all capital letters or underscored.

CONFIDENTIAL   or   <u>Confidential</u>

(3) INSIDE ADDRESS

The inside address starts four spaces below the date line (or two below the mailing or in-house notation, if applicable) and includes the name of the person to whom you are writing; the name of the company, if applicable; the street address; and the name of the city, state, and ZIP code.

Whether or not the title should appear on the same line as the name will be determined by the length. Try to square the inside address as much as possible.

The two-letter state abbreviation is used for the inside address. (See the end of this section for a complete listing.) The state name should be written out if appearing in the body of the letter.

> Mr. Edward J. Cox
> Cox Communications
> 370 State Street
> Port Chester, NY 10573

The inside address should always consist of at least three lines. When you have a company with no street address, such as would be located in a very small town, place the state and ZIP code under the city.

> Dolores Ramsey & Assoc.
> Small Town
> State, 00000

NOTE: Refer to the chapters entitled "Capitalization" and "Numbers" for further information regarding the inside address.

(4) ATTENTION LINE

The attention line is used when you are writing directly to the company and want the letter directed to a particular person and/or department. The salutation, therefore, is always *Gentlemen*.

> ATTENTION ELSIE HERSCH (capitals with no
>   colon)
> Attention Personnel Manager
> Attention: Accounting Department

The attention line is placed on the envelope as follows:

P & M Construction
  Company
345 Madison Avenue
Columbus, OH 43004
  ↓ 2 *(double space)*
Attention: Paul Sharfin
  ↓ 2
	P & M Construction
	  Company
	Attention: Paul Sharfin
	345 Madison Avenue
	Columbus, OH 43004

(5) SALUTATION

The salutation is placed two lines below the address or attention line (whichever appears last) and should correspond directly to the first line of the inside address. With mixed punctuation, a colon follows the salutation. With open punctuation, no mark follows the salutation or the complimentary closing.

Mr. John Smith	Dear Mr. Smith: Dear John: (informal)
Mrs. Joan Smith	Dear Mrs. Smith: Dear Joan: (informal)

Ms. Jean Smith	Dear Ms. Smith: Dear Jean: (informal)
Mr. and Mrs. John Smith	Dear Mr. and Mrs. Smith: Dear John and Joan: (informal)
Messrs. Max and Harry Lorenz	Dear Messrs. Lorenz: Dear Max and Harry: (informal)
Mmes. Ethel and Marilyn Lorenz	Dear Mmes. Lorenz: Dear Ethel and Marilyn: (informal)
The Comptroller	Dear Sir: (male) Dear Madam: (female)
A & D Shoppes	Gentlemen: Ladies: (if corporation of women)

NOTE: Refer to chapter 16, "Forms of Address," for government officials, military personnel, religious officials and education officials.

(6) SUBJECT LINE

This is considered part of the letter, not the heading; therefore, it should always be placed two spaces below the salutation. The purpose of the subject line is to direct the reader to the theme of the letter. The subject line can be in all capital letters, or underscored, or neither. The horizontal placement will depend on the letter style.

SUBJECT: ACCOUNT NO. 8198
Subject: Policy No. 721135
Re: Introductory Magazine Offer
In re: Invoice No. 343635

(7) BODY OR MESSAGE

The body of the letter is generally single spaced with double spacing between paragraphs.

a. The opening paragraph is relatively short and introduces the letter.
b. The middle paragraph(s) support the opening and/or provide additional information.
c. The final paragraph is short and serves as a summation, request, suggestion, or look to the future.

(8) COMPLIMENTARY CLOSING

The complimentary closing appears two vertical lines below the last typewritten line, and only the first letter of the first word is capitalized.

With mixed punctuation, a comma follows the closing. With open punctuation, no mark follows.

formal: Yours truly, Very truly yours, Yours very truly, Respectfully, Respectfully yours,

informal: Sincerely, Sincerely yours, Cordially, Cordially yours,

personal: Best wishes, As always, Regards, Kindest regards,

NOTE: Refer to chapter 16, "Forms of Address," for government officials, military personnel, religious officials, and education officials.

(9) SIGNATURE LINE

Horizontal placement depends on the letter. Personal signatures can be handled in any of the following ways:

Very truly yours,

[signature: Christine Nicolucci]

Secretary to Mr. Lorenz

Very truly yours,

[signature: Harry Lorenz]

Harry Lorenz
Assistant Manager

Very truly yours,

[signature: Christine Nicolucci]

Ms. Christine Nicolucci

Very truly yours,

(Ms.) *[signature: Christine Nicolucci]*

Christine Nicolucci

Unless both the name and title are short, it is best to separate them on different lines, with no comma. Allow at least four vertical spaces between the complimentary closing and the typed name so that a person with a large handwriting will have room for his/her signature.

Some companies prefer to have their names appear in this portion of the letter.

Very truly yours,

↓2

A & G PIE COMPANY

↓4

V. Gasparre, President

Very truly yours,

↓2

A & G PIE COMPANY

↓4

V. Gasparre
President

The comma is used *only* when the title appears on the same line as the name.

(10) REFERENCE INITIALS

The initials are always typed at the left margin two lines below the writer's name and/or title. They include the writer's initials (first) and the typist's initials (second) or the typist's initials only.

HLorenz/jt	HL/JT
HL:jt	jt

Reference initials are omitted from personal letters and from letters that you are writing on behalf of your employer and signing yourself.

(11) ENCLOSURE NOTATION

The enclosure notation appears on the line directly below the reference initials when anything is being sent along with the letter.

Enclosure	1 Enc.
Enc.	Enclosure 2
Encls.	Enc. (2)
Enclosures	Enclosure:
	1. Purchase Order No. 123
1 Enclosure	2. Check No. 345

In some offices, when something is attached rather than enclosed, the word *Attachment* will appear in place of *Enclosure*.

(12) COPY NOTATION

When a copy of the letter is sent to a third person, a notation to that effect is made directly below the enclosure notation or reference initials.

CC: A. Karp   cc: A. Karp
CC A Karp   Copy to: A. Karp

The abbreviation "CC" or "cc" stands for "carbon copy." Even though most offices now use photocopies, this abbreviation is still in general use.

If the writer does not want to apprise the addressee that a third party will be receiving a copy of the letter, a blind copy notation is made on the office copy and third party copy *only*. No notation is made on the original.

BCC: M. Cole   bcc M. Cole
BC: M. Cole   bc M. Cole

(13) POSTSCRIPT

A postscript should be used sparingly because it could be interpreted as an afterthought and indicate a lack of organization on the part of the writer. Sometimes, however, it is used for emphasis.

To include a postscript, merely double space after the last notation and begin your message. The *P.S.* notation is no longer used.

jt
Enclosure

I will call you for lunch next Monday!

The first of the sample letters that begin on the following page shows the standard letter parts just explained. The numbers in parentheses on the letter correspond to the part numbers given above.

LIGHTING & DECORATING, Inc.

RENTALS & INSTALLATIONS

Back Drops — Booths — Wiring for Hotel and Trade Shows

April 12, 19-- ———————————————————— (1) Date Line

CERTIFIED MAIL ———————————————————— (2) Mailing Notation

• SEARCHLIGHTS

• SOUND

• BALL FIELD
  LIGHTING

• DISPLAY
  LIGHTING

• FLOOD
  LIGHTING

• FURNITURE
  RENTAL

• N. J. STATE
  LICENSE #3110

Marric Enterprises ——————————————— (3) Inside Address
Attention Thomas James ——————————— (4) Attention Line
24 Blazer Way
Spring Valley, NY 10977

Gentlemen: ———————————————————————— (5) Salutation

Subject: Hunting and Fishing Contract ————— (6) Subject Line

I am enclosing the contract we agreed upon stipulating
all the terms and conditions of the hunting and
fishing show that will take place at the Besen
Community College Field House during the week of   (7) Body
May 1.   or Message

Can we meet for lunch on either Monday, Tuesday,
or Wednesday of next week to finalize the details?
If neither of these dates is convenient, please call
my office so that we can arrange a mutually convenient time.

Sincerely yours, ——————————————————— (8) Complimentary Closing

LIGHTING & DECORATING, INC.

Noel Christie, President ——————————————— (9) Signature Line

sll ——————————————————————————————— (10) Reference Line
Enclosure ————————————————————————— (11) Enclosure Notation
cc: Besen Community College ————————————— (12) Carbon Copy Notation

The ski show contract will be ready next week.————— (13) Postscript

143 East Railway Avenue, Paterson, NJ 07503   (201) 345-1250

ATLAS FIVE AND TEN INC.

HILDE AND HELMUT FEILER
—

179 MAIN STREET
FORT LEE, N. J. 07024
(201) 947-2999

February 20, 19--

Mr. and Mrs. Benjamin Swartz
138 Tapia Drive
Paramus, NJ 07652

Dear Mr. and Mrs. Swartz:

Re: Account No. 94132

We are delighted to welcome you to our Atlas family of
charge customers. Your application for a charge account
has been approved, and our staff is waiting to make your
shopping a satisfying and pleasurable experience.

On the tenth of each month you will receive a statement of your
purchases, and you will have until the twenty-fifth of the
month to make your payment. From the outstanding credit
reputation you have earned, we are certain that your payments
will be made promptly, thus avoiding any service charges.

We are taking this opportunity to send you our latest catalog
so that you can take advantage of our easy shop-at-home
service.

Thank you for giving us the opportunity to show you why Atlas
has earned the fine reputation for high-quality merchandise
and superior service. Remember: "If we don't have it; you
don't need it."

Very truly yours,

ATLAS FIVE AND TEN INC.

Michael Feiler, President

sll
Enclosure

FULL BLOCK STYLE
This modern letter style is becoming more and more popular.
Everything begins at the left margin; nothing is indented.

OFFICE
ORegon 5-2043

Max H. Lorenz

PUBLIC ACCOUNTANT
408 WEST 14th STREET
NEW YORK, N. Y. 10014

ANSWERING SERVICE
BA 7-5816

November 14, 19--

Mr. Warren Bergstein
Business Club
103 Samuel Lane
Grasmere, NY 10305

Dear Mr. Bergstein:

Subject: New Tax Laws for 19--

It is with great pleasure that I accept your
invitation to speak to your membership about
"New Tax Laws for 19--" at your January meeting.

I would appreciate your having available an
overhead projector, a chalkboard, and a table in
front of the room where I can display literature
and current tax forms for distribution. Also,
please let me know approximately how many
members will be in attendance.

Immediately following my presentation, I will
gladly entertain any questions your members may
have, either of a general or personal nature.
I am certain that your members will find the
information both useful and informative.

Thank you for giving me the opportunity to address
your organization.

Sincerely yours,

Max H. Lorenz

ML/el

MODIFIED BLOCK STYLE

This traditional letter style is the most commonly used. Everything
begins at the left margin with the exception of the date line and
complimentary closing. Both start at the center or slightly to the
right of center.

April 15, 19--

Mr. and Mrs. Harry Lorenz
36 Lincoln Road
Monroe, NY 10950

Dear Mr. and Mrs. Lorenz:

        Re: Scholarship Awards

        On behalf of the faculty and staff at
Taylor Business Institute, I wish to congratulate
your daughters, Jacqueline and Nicole, for winning
one-half tuition scholarships for the accounting
program.

        You can be extremely proud of their results
as there were many other competitors who took the
exam in your area.

        Our early registration will be held on
Saturday, May 3 from 9 AM to 2 PM, and we look
forward to welcoming Jacqueline and Nicole to our
Taylor family.

        Sincerely,

        Marilyn Sarch, Dean

sll

291 Buehler Place at Route 17, Paramus, New Jersey 07652

SEMIBLOCK STYLE

This letter style is identical to the modified block style, except each
paragraph is indented five to seven spaces from the left margin and
the subject line is centered.

Real World Counseling Service
P.O. Box 502
Nanuet, New York 10954

(914) 352-3240
(914) 352-9113

April 21, 19--

Mr. Brian Karen
35 Amy Court
Highland Falls, NY 10928

RE: MARVIN BRIAN, FILE NO. 5857

I greatly value you as a client and would like
to be of service to you in the future should the
need arise.

Your son Marvin has successfully completed the
career counseling program designed especially for
him; and, as a result, is now gainfully and
happily employed. Yet, you have made no effort
to pay any part of the $250 which has been due and
owing since January.

As a business person, I know that you appreciate
those of your customers who meet their obligations
promptly.

Won't you, therefore, send me your check for the
full amount of $250 and retain the good credit
standing you have earned.

JANICE TEISCH, DIRECTOR

sll

SIMPLIFIED STYLE

This letter style is written in full block with the salutation and complimentary closing omitted. The subject line appears in all capital letters three lines below the inside address and three lines above the body. The writer's name appears four lines below the final paragraph, also in all capital letters.

This streamlined letter style has been recommended by the Administrative Management Society and is expected to be the trend of the future as it is less time consuming, thereby cutting costs.

Two-Page Letters

When typing a two-page letter, use letterhead for the first page and plain bond paper of the same color and weight for the second page.

When you divide a paragraph between pages, at least two lines must remain on the first page and two lines be carried to the following page. A three-line paragraph cannot be divided, and you *cannot* carry the complimentary closing to a second page without having at least two lines above it.

The heading on the second page should be as follows:

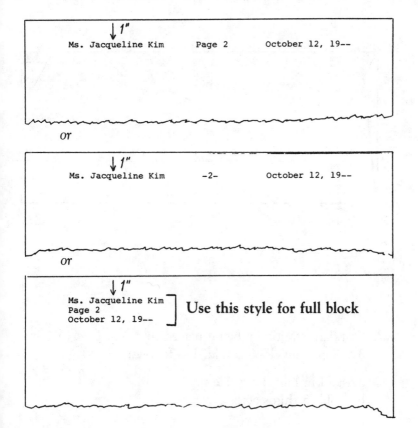

FOLDING THE LETTER

1. Standard (8½ by 11 inch) stationery being placed in a
   No. 10 (9½ by 4⅛ inch) envelope, Monarch (7¼ by 10½
   inch) stationery being placed in a No. 7 (7½ by 3⅞ inch)
   envelope, or Baronial (5½ by 8½ inch) stationery being
   placed in a No. 6¾ (6½ by 3⅝ inch) envelope folded
   as follows:

   a. Fold the bottom of the letter approximately one-
      third up and make a crease.
   b. Fold the top one-third down and make a crease.

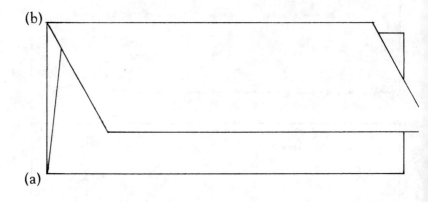

2. Standard stationery being placed in a No. 6¾ (6½ by
   3⅝ inch) envelope is folded as follows:

   a. Fold in half, long side up.
   b. Fold in thirds across.

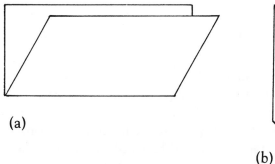

(a)

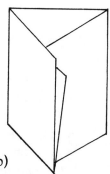

(b)

3. Stationery being placed in a window envelope will be folded as follows:

  a. Fold the bottom of the letter approximately one-third up and make a crease.
  b. Fold the top one-third back and make a crease. The inside address should be on the outside and placed in the envelope so that it is visible through the window.

(a)

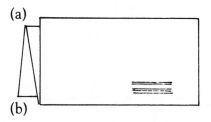

(b)

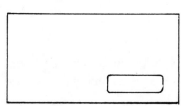

Envelopes

ADDRESSING THE ENVELOPE

1. The address is single spaced in the block style. The address should appear on the envelope as it appears on the inside address.
2. All in-house notations (personal, attention, confidential, hold, please forward) should be typed two to three lines below the return address and should align with the left margin.
3. All postal notations (special delivery, certified mail, registered mail, air mail, by messenger) should be typed under where the stamp will be placed (approximately nine lines from the top.)

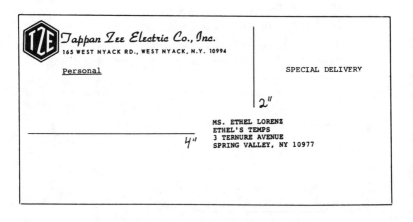

No. 10 envelope

4. Optical character readers (OCR) are now expediting the mail in many large cities, and the use of the OCR is

becoming widespread. The Post Office is, therefore, suggesting that the following guidelines be followed for the increased accuracy and speed of mail delivery.

a. The name and address should be typed in all capital letters with no punctuation. (Note the abbreviation of AVE, ST, BLVD, RD, etc.)

STANLEY ALPERT
ROCKLAND PHYSICAL THERAPY SERVICE
55 OLD TURNPIKE RD
NANUET NY 10954

b. If the addressee used both a street address and a post office box, the line directly above the city, state and ZIP code is where the letter will be delivered.

c. If a room or suite number is used, it should immediately follow the street address on the same line.

56 FIFTH ST ROOM 304

d. The five-digit ZIP code must be used. ZIP code directories are available at the post office or can be purchased at any bookstore. The nine-digit ZIP code is recommended by the post office to make mail handling and delivery more efficient. Post offices have listings for the last four digits in their respective states.

e. The two-letter state abbreviation should be used on all mail.

f. Names of cities, towns, and commonly used streets are also abbreviated.

Memorial Drive = MEM DR

Two-Letter State Abbreviations

Alabama	AL	Missouri	MO
Alaska	AK	Montana	MT
Arizona	AZ	Nebraska	NE
Arkansas	AR	Nevada	NV
California	CA	New Hampshire	NH
Canal Zone	CZ	New Jersey	NJ
Colorado	CO	New Mexico	NM
Connecticut	CT	New York	NY
Delaware	DE	North Carolina	NC
District of		North Dakota	ND
Columbia	DC	Ohio	OH
Florida	FL	Oklahoma	OK
Georgia	GA	Oregon	OR
Guam	GU	Pennsylvania	PA
Hawaii	HI	Puerto Rico	PR
Idaho	ID	Rhode Island	RI
Illinois	IL	South Carolina	SC
Indiana	IN	South Dakota	SD
Iowa	IA	Tennessee	TN
Kansas	KS	Texas	TX
Kentucky	KY	Utah	UT
Louisiana	LA	Vermont	VT
Maine	ME	Virginia	VA
Maryland	MD	Virgin Islands	VI
Massachusetts	MA	Washington	WA
Michigan	MI	West Virginia	WV
Minnesota	MN	Wisconsin	WI
Mississippi	MS	Wyoming	WY

When addressing foreign mail, enter the country name as the last line of the address block, two line spaces below the city line.

Interoffice Memos

The main purpose of the interoffice memo is to transmit ideas, decisions, and suggestions to another member or members of your organization. If an organization uses memos frequently, it will generally have the forms printed. The forms can be half sheets or full sheets, depending on the length of the message.

On a memo you:

Omit	**Retain**
inside address	body or message
salutation	reference initials
complimentary closing	enclosure notation
signature	carbon copy notation

1. Start the body of the memo three spaces below the heading.
2. Align the left margin with the typewritten portion of the heading, and set the right margin so that it is equal to the left.
3. Single space the paragraphs in block style, double spacing between each paragraph.
4. When typing a memo on a blank sheet of paper, start 1½ inches from the top. Any of the following headings may be used:

To:	TO:	
From:	FROM:	or
Date:	DATE:	
Subject:	SUBJECT:	

or

Date:	Date:	
To:	TO:	
From:	FROM:	
Subject:	SUBJECT:	

or

5. Double space between each item in the heading, and proceed as for a printed memo form.

A sample memo appears on page 191.

Postal Cards

Because a postal card does not allow much room for a message, the inside address, complimentary closing, and written signature are often omitted from the side that carries the message.

Both sides of a sample postal card appear on page 192.

Local Union No. 363   •   Rockland and Orange Counties, New York
60 PHILLIPS HILL ROAD, NEW CITY, NEW YORK 10956 • (914) 634-4601

TO: The Executive Board

FROM: Cosmo E. Damiani, Business Manager

DATE: September 16, 19--

SUBJECT: Insurance Plan

Please be advised that there will be a brief meeting on Thursday, September 22, at 2 PM, to discuss the following:

1. Changes in Insurance, and

2. New Employee Benefits.

All are expected to attend.

CED

sl

NOTE: Some executives choose either to sign or to initial the bottom of the memo.

Joan Sheridan
30 Besen Parkway
Suffern, NY 10901

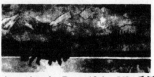

America the Beautiful   USA **15**

2"

2"

Ms. Sheryl N. Thomas
25 West Funston Avenue
Spring Valley, NY 10977

©USPS 1988

December 2, 19--

Dear Ms. Thomas:

Please be advised that the date of our
meeting is being changed to Friday,
December 9 at 2 PM.

If you are able to arrive a half hour
early, I will be able to brief you.

Joan Sheridan

CHAPTER 11

REPORTS, MINUTES, AND ITINERARIES

Reports, Styling, Tables and Charts, Footnotes, Bibliographies, Minutes, Itineraries

Reports

Reports represent the prime method an executive has for obtaining and communicating information. Reports are written in the third person and deal with facts, letting the reader form his or her own opinion.

A report can take the form of an outline, a memorandum, or a formal report.

OUTLINES

Some reports are written in outline form; some use the outline as a preliminary for a more formal report. The outline separates the data into divisions and subdivisions for easy identification.

In the sample outline on page 195, notice the use of capitalization for the divisions and subdivisions.

1. For the heading, use a standard style or a spread heading.
   a. For a *standard heading*, start at the center point (50

on an elite and 42 on a pica) and backspace once for every two letters and spaces. Then type the heading normally.

STANDARD HEADING

b. For a *spread heading*, start at the center point and backspace once for every letter and space. Then type heading leaving one space between letters and three spaces between words.

S P R E A D   H E A D I N G

2. The secondary headings (A, B, C) can be either single or double spaced, depending on the length of the outline. They always, however, start a double space below the major division.
3. Set the tab for each subdivision, which is indented four spaces.

MEMOS

For reports prepared in memo form, refer to the chapter "Letters, Memos and Postal Cards."

FORMAL REPORTS

1. If you are preparing a formal report that will be reproduced, be certain that the cover page, table of contents, first page of each chapter, appendices, and index appear on odd-numbered, right-hand pages. You can ensure this by inserting blank left-hand pages where necessary. For example, if Chapter One ends on a right-hand page, the next left-hand page must be blank in order for Chapter Two to begin on a right-hand page.

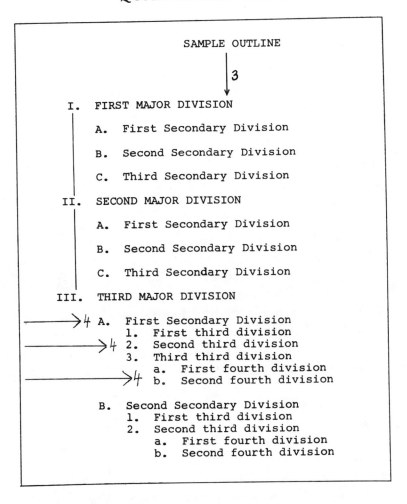

```
                    SAMPLE OUTLINE

                            3

  I.  FIRST MAJOR DIVISION

      A.  First Secondary Division

      B.  Second Secondary Division

      C.  Third Secondary Division

 II.  SECOND MAJOR DIVISION

      A.  First Secondary Division

      B.  Second Secondary Division

      C.  Third Secondary Division

III.  THIRD MAJOR DIVISION

      A.  First Secondary Division
          1.  First third division
          2.  Second third division
          3.  Third third division
              a.  First fourth division
              b.  Second fourth division

      B.  Second Secondary Division
          1.  First third division
          2.  Second third division
              a.  First fourth division
              b.  Second fourth division
```

2. Many executives require a draft of the report so that it can be revised and polished. A draft should be prepared with double or triple spacing so as to allow room for editing. Unless the draft is to be distributed to several people, it is unnecessary to make copies.

3. The formal report can contain any combination of the following:

title page	method
table of contents	conclusions
letter of transmittal	recommendations
purpose	synopsis
scope and/or limit	bibliography
hypothesis	appendix(es)

Styling

MARGINS

1. When a report is to be bound at the top, use one-inch side margins and a one-inch bottom margin. The first page should have a two-inch top margin, and all ensuing pages a one-inch top margin.
2. When a report is to be bound at the left, leave one and a half inches for the left margin. All other margins remain the same. For centering, the middle point becomes 54 on an elite and 46 in a pica.

PARAGRAPHS

1. Paragraphs should be indented five to seven spaces from the left margin.
2. The text in a formal report will generally be double spaced, with double spacing between paragraphs. When a text is single spaced, also double space between paragraphs.

PAGINATION

1. The first page of a report (or chapter of a report) is generally not numbered.
2. All subsequent pages should be numbered four lines from the top at the right margin for a left-bound report. For a

top-bound report, the number should be centered on the seventh line from the bottom.

QUOTED MATERIAL

Long quoted passages are idented five spaces from the left and right margins and single spaced. The quotation marks are then omitted.

For other uses of the quotation mark, refer to the "Punctuation" chapter.

TITLE PAGE

Although many styles are acceptable, the title page generally contains the name of the report; by whom it was prepared; the office, school, or institution from which it originated; the date on which it was presented; and, in many cases, to whom it was presented. (See page 198 for example.)

TITLE PAGE

AN EXPERIMENTAL STUDY TO DETERMINE THE

EFFECT OF THE SPELLING TEST ON

THE ABILITY OF STUDENTS TO SPELL

Presented to

the Faculty of the

Department of Business Education

and Office Systems Administration

Montclair State College

by

Sheryl Lorenz

B.S., Saint Thomas Aquinas College

December 19XX

The table of contents lists subject headings and their respective pages.

PAGE 1

The first page of your report is not numbered and starts on line 13 (two inches from the top). The margins will be one inch on the right and one inch on the left. The report should end one inch from the bottom of the page.

2"

INTRODUCTION TO THE PROBLEM

Chapter 1

"Johnny can't read"; Johnny can't spell either. The researcher and colleagues have a consensus of opinion that students graduating from our high school systems are deficient in the area of spelling. This is evidenced by the lack of spelling ability in transcriptions, in sentences, in basic English drills, and in business subjects. At the postsecondary level of a private business school, the students have one year to hone their spelling skills prior to entering the world of business.

Many of today's students were educated when basics were forsaken, and the emphasis was on creativity. Educators, viewing this alarming deficiency in the area of language arts in general, are reaffirming the importance of a back-to-basics education. It is, therefore, the responsibility of each educator to seek ways to overcome this problem.

The researcher would like to determine whether the use of weekly spelling tests will increase the spelling ability of students in a private postsecondary business school.

This problem will determine whether it is worthwhile for teachers to administer weekly spelling tests in order to improve the spelling ability of students.

1"   1"

BIBLIOGRAPHY

This is a listing of all sources of reference and starts two inches from the top. The bibliography has one-inch side margins and five additional spaces are indented for added lines. The form is the reverse of a paragraph.

2"

BIBLIOGRAPHY

--> Helphill, Phyllis David. Business Communications With   <--
         Writing Improvement Exercises. Englewood Cliffs, NJ: 1"
   1"   Prentice-Hall, 1958.

      Tuckman, Bruce W. Conducting Educational Research. 2d ed.
         New York: Harcourt Brace Jovanovich, 1978.

      Warriner, John and Sheila Y. Laws. English Grammar and Com-
         munication. New York: Harcourt Brace Jovanovich, 1973.

Tables and Charts

UNRULED TABLE

WEATHER TABLE
↓ 2
Week of March 1
↓ 3

Day	Weather
↓2	↓2
Sunday	Sunny
Monday	Sunny
Tuesday	Rainy
Wednesday	Rainy
Thursday	Cloudy
Friday	Sunny
Saturday	Cloudy

RULED TABLE

WEATHER TABLE
↓ 2
Week of March 1
↓ 3

Day	Weather
↓2	↓2
Sunday	Sunny
Monday	Sunny
Tuesday	Rainy
Wednesday	Rainy
Thursday	Cloudy
Friday	Sunny
Saturday	Cloudy

Works Cited and Works Referenced

Whenever you are using material from another source (facts, opinions, quotes), you must give credit to the source. This is a matter of good judgment as well as ethics. We are very much accustomed to using the terms "Footnotes" and "Bibliography," but those terms seem to have gone the way of the dinosaur.

Works Cited (otherwise known as "footnote") lists all works quoted or referenced in your manuscript. This item now appears at the end of your manuscript, not on the bottom of each page as you may be accustomed to seeing it. *Works Consulted* (otherwise known as "bibliography") lists all references used for your research. Each of these is double-spaced for easy reading. When using both at the conclusion of a manuscript, Works Cited is listed first, followed by Works Consulted.

GENERAL GUIDELINES

An entry is double-spaced and lists three main divisions—author, title and publication information. Each is followed by a period and two spaces, and is indented after the first line of entry. If you are citing a book, list the information in the following order: author's name; title of publication; name of editor; edition; number of volumes; name of series; place of publication, name of publisher, date of publication; page number; supplementary bibliographic information and annotation.

Book:	Lindsell, Sheryl L. *Word Processing Mastery for Everyone.* New York: Arco Publishing, Inc., 1982.
Magazine:	Lindsell, Sheryl L. "Title of Article." *Publication,* April. 1988: 24.
Computer Software:	*Wordstar.* Release 3.3. Computer software. Micropro, 1983.
Proceedings of Conference:	Humanistic Scholarship in America. Proc. of a Conference on the Princeton Studies in the Humanities. 5-6 Nov. 1965, Princeton: Princeton, U. 1966.
Chart:	*Grammar and Punctuation.* Chart. Grand Haven: School Zone, 1980.
Lectures:	Lindsell, Sheryl L. Address. The Art of Communications. RCWN Convention. Suffern, XX April, 1988.

If you prepare manuscripts frequently, you may wish to consider purchasing a copy of the *MLA Style Manual,* published by the Modern Language Association.

Minutes

The notes you take at a meeting must be accurate, but they do not have to be verbatim. If the meeting is to be very formal, your company might want a record of every word; they will probably allow a tape recorder to aid you, but you must obtain permission to use it.

If you are not accustomed to taking minutes, acquaint yourself with minutes of previous meetings so that you can apply the format.

If you are expected to conduct a meeting, review parliamentary procedure as clearly explained in *Robert's Rules of Order Newly Revised*, the bible for conducting business meetings.

Keep in mind the following:

1. Record the date, time, and place of the meeting, and all those who were present. Also note the time the meeting commenced and adjourned.
2. Sit near the presiding officer so that you hear everything clearly and accurately.
3. Remain constantly alert so that each time a new topic is introduced, you are prepared to record the name of the person who introduced it, seconded it, and the main points covered.
4. Use your judgment; never expect any member of the meeting to tell you what is important. If in doubt, include it.
5. Record the name of each person who proposes any action, opinion, or plan.
6. Take verbatim notes on resolutions, amendments, decisions, and conclusions.
7. Have paper clips handy (attached to your notebook) so that you can tag any items on which action is to be taken after the meeting. This will aid you in picking out these duties before transcribing your notes.
8. Make certain that you have heard everything clearly. If unsure, ask for the unclear portion to be repeated. Names, amounts of money, and dates are of extreme importance. (See example on page 206.)

DIRECTOR'S MEETING

August 15, 19--

The regular monthly meeting of The Marric Corporation Board of Directors was held on Monday, August 15, 19--, at 9 AM, in the company boardroom. President Marc Allen presided.

The following members were present: Eric Laurence, Thomas James, Jeff Teisch, Steven Teisch, Martha Rones, and Ethel Lorenz.

The minutes of the July 14, 19--, meeting were read by the Secretary and approved.

President Allen suggested that a feasibility study to determine the need for a computer system be instituted. The matter was tabled, and President Allen requested that the members be prepared to vote on such a study at the September meeting.

Eric Laurence requested that the advertising budget be increased by 10 percent in order to reach this year's quota. The request was approved unanimously because the Advertising Department had cut expenses in certain areas.

Thomas James reported that sales on the new Model 30A fishing rods are better than expected. The line is expected to be expanded.

The next meeting will be held on Tuesday, September 15, 19--. The meeting was adjourned at 10:30 AM.

Respectfully submitted,
Ethel Lorenz, Secretary

Itineraries

When making travel arrangements (domestic or international), it is best to contact a travel agent. There is no out-of-pocket fee involved. The travel agent can plan an itinerary, making all the travel arrangements and supplying whatever information might be needed. The names of accredited travel agents are available from ASTA.

> American Society of Travel Agents
> 666 5th Ave
> 12th floor
> New York, NY 10103

Be prepared to supply the travel agent with the following information:
1. employer's name, company, business phone, and possibly home phone
2. cities to be visited
3. dates and times of arrivals and departures
4. transportation preference (mode and class)
5. lodging preference (many prefer certain hotels)

Next, it will be necessary to prepare an itinerary—a chronological, easy-to-read schedule of daily events. The itinerary should contain:
1. date, time, and place of departure
2. mode of transportation (confirmed)
3. date, time, and place of arrival
4. lodging accommodations (confirmed)
5. appointments and any information pertinent thereto
6. date, time, and place of departure
7. mode of transportation (confirmed)
8. date, time, and place of return

ITINERARY FOR ETHEL LORENZ

From May 1 to May 6

Monday
May 1

9:30 AM EST   Leave Newark Airport via TWA, Flight No. 205
               (tickets in envelope)

10:30 PST   Arrive in Las Vegas - Reservations at MGM
               Grand Hotel (confirmation attached)

7:00   Dinner with Andrea Teisch - phone her prior
               to meeting at (702) 123-7654

Tuesday
May 2

9 AM   Convention at MGM Grand (program attached)

Evening   Free

Wednesday
May 3

10:30 AM   Leave Las Vegas Airport via Western Airlines
               Flight No. 145 (tickets in envelope)

11:05 AM   Arrive San Francisco. Hotel reservations at
               Sheraton Inn (confirmation attached)

Thursday
May 4

12 noon   Address San Francisco Bar Association in
               Cypress Room of Hyatt-Regency (notes on 3 x 5
               cards in briefcase)

Friday
May 5   No scheduled activities

Saturday
May 6

9 AM   Leave San Francisco Airport, Flight No. 56
               (tickets in envelope)

5 PM EST   Arrive Newark Airport. Limousine will be
               waiting.

                                        Enjoy your trip!

Toll-Free Numbers for Airlines, Car Rentals and Lodging

Airlines:

American Airlines	1-800-433-7300
Australian Airlines	1-800-922-5122
British Airways	1-800-247-9297
Continental Airlines	1-800-525-0280
Delta Airlines	1-800-221-1212
Lufthansa Airlines	1-800-645-3880
Mexicana Airlines	1-800-531-7921
Northwest Airlines	1-800-225-2525
Piedmont	1-800-251-5720
Qantas Airways	1-800-227-4500
TWA	1-800-221-2000
United Airlines	1-800-241-6522
US AIR	1-800-428-4322

Car Rentals:

Alamo Rent A Car	1-800-327-9633
Avis Rent A Car	1-800-331-1212
Budget Car & Truck Rental	1-800-527-0700
Dollar Rent A Car	1-800-228-9987
General Rent A Car	1-800-327-7607
Hertz Rent A Car	1-800-654-3131
National Car Rental	1-800-344-6338
Thrifty Car Rental	1-800-367-2277

Lodging:

Americana Inns	1-800-228-3278
Barclay Hotel	1-800-327-0200
Best Western	1-800-528-1234

Budget Inns	1-800-334-9333
Courtyard by Marriott	1-800-321-2211
Days Inns of America	1-800-241-2340
Four Seasons Hotels	1-800-828-1188
Helmsley Hotels	1-800-221-4982
Hilton International	1-800-445-8667
Holiday Inn	1-800-465-4329
Howard Johnson	1-800-654-2000
Hyatt Hotels	1-800-228-9000
Marriott Hotels	1-800-228-9290
Meridian Hotels	1-800-223-9918
Omni Int'l Hotels	1-800-421-5500
Quality Inns	1-800-228-5151
Ramada Inn	1-800-228-2828
Red Carpet Inns	1-800-251-1962
Ritz-Carlton-Boston	1-800-323-7500
Ritz-Carlton-Chicago	1-800-621-9606
Sheraton Hotels	1-800-325-3535
Sonesta Hotels	1-800-343-7170
Stouffer Hotels	1-800-468-3571
Tradeway Inns	1-800-631-0182
TraveLodge	1-800-255-3050
Western Hotels/Resorts	1-800-228-3000

It is now possible to make airline and hotel reservations electronically through the Official Airline Guide Electronics Edition (OAGEE).

CHAPTER 12

FORMS OF ADDRESS

Government Officials, Military Personnel,
Religious Officials, Education Officials

Government Officials

Person	Salutation	Closing
The President	Dear Mr./Mrs./Ms. President: Mr./Mrs./Ms. President:	Respectfully yours,
The Vice-President	Dear Mr./Mrs./Ms. Vice-President: Mr./Mrs./Ms. Vice-President:	Respectfully yours,
Chief Justice	Dear Mr./Madam Chief Justice: Sir/Madam:	Very truly yours, Sincerely yours,
Cabinet Officers	Dear Mr./Madam Secretary: The Honorable...:	Very truly yours, Sincerely yours,
Senators	Dear Senator...: The Honorable...:	Very truly yours, Sincerely yours,
Representative	The Honorable...: Sir/Madam:	Very truly yours, Sincerely yours,
Governor	Dear Governor...: Sir/Madam:	Respectfully yours, Very sincerely yours,
State Senator	Dear Senator...: Sir/Madam:	Very truly yours, Sincerely yours,
State Representative	Dear Mr./Mrs./Ms....: Sir/Madam:	Very truly yours, Sincerely yours,
Mayor	Dear Mayor...: Dear Sir/Madam:	Very truly yours, Sincerely yours,

Person	Salutation	Closing
Ambassador	Dear Mr./Madam Ambassador: Sir/Madam:	Very truly yours, Sincerely yours,
Minister	Dear Mr./Madam Minister: Sir/Madam:	Very truly yours, Sincerely yours,

Military Personnel

General, USA*	Dear General...: Sir/Madam:	Very truly yours, Sincerely yours,
Lieutenant General	Dear General...: Sir/Madam:	Very truly yours, Sincerely yours,
Colonel	Dear Colonel:	Very truly yours, Sincerely yours,
Major	Dear Major...:	Very truly yours, Sincerely yours,
Captain	Dear Captain...:	Very truly yours, Sincerely yours,
Admiral, USN	Dear Admiral...:	Very truly yours, Sincerely yours,
Chaplain	Dear Chaplain...:	Very truly yours, Sincerely yours,

Religious Officials

Cardinal	Dear Cardinal...: Your Eminence:	Respectfully, Sincerely yours,
Archbishop	Dear Archbishop...: Your Excellency:	Respectfully, Sincerely yours,

*United States Army.

Person	Salutation	Closing
Bishop	Dear Bishop...: Your Excellency:	Respectfully, Sincerely yours,
Monsignor	Dear Monsignor...: Right Reverend Monsignor	Respectfully yours, Sincerely yours,
Priest	Reverend Father: Dear Father...:	Respectfully, Sincerely yours,
Mother Superior	Dear Reverend Mother: Dear Mother...:	Respectfully, Sincerely yours,
Nun	Dear Sister...: Dear Sister:	Respectfully, Sincerely yours,
Reverend	Reverend Sir:	Respectfully yours, Sincerely yours,
Rabbi	Dear Rabbi...: Sir:	Respectfully yours, Sincerely yours,

Education Officials

Person	Salutation	Closing
President	Dear Dr....: Sir/Madam:	Very truly yours, Sincerely yours,
Dean	Dear Dean...: Dear Sir/Madam:	Very truly yours, Sincerely yours,
Professor	Dear Professor...: Dear Sir/Madam:	Very truly yours, Sincerely yours,
Instructor	Dear Mr....: Dear Sir/Madam:	Very truly yours, Sincerely yours,

CHAPTER 13

POSTAL AND OTHER MAIL SERVICES

Domestic Mail, Special Services, International Mail, Hints for Reducing Postal Expenses, Special Services, Electronic Mail

Postal rates are subject to change; therefore, this chapter will be limited to the services that are available, not the rates. (Current rates can be obtained from any local post office.)

Domestic Mail

Domestic mail encompasses mail sent within the United States and between the United States, its territories, and its possessions. It includes Army-Air Force (APO) and Navy (FPO [the *F* stands for *Fleet*]) post offices and any mail sent to the United Nations in New York City.

First-Class Mail includes sealed letters (typewritten, handwritten, carbon copy, or photocopy), postcards, business reply cards and letters, checks, and greeting cards that measure at least 3½ by 5 inches in diameter. Any piece of first-class mail will be returned unless sufficient postage is attached.

When a large manila envelope is being sent first class, this designation should be marked on the front and back of the envelope. Special envelopes with green diamond borders are intended for first-class mailing.

Second-Class Mail includes newspapers, magazines, and periodicals. Publishers and news agencies wishing to mail second class are required to obtain permits from the United States Postal Service and must adhere to all postal rules and regulations.

Third-Class Mail includes circulars, books, catalogs, seeds, cuttings, bulbs, roots, and plants weighing less than 16 ounces. Special rates apply to bulk mailing and to books, records, films, and various educational materials.

Fourth-Class Mail, also known as parcel post, should not be confused with the United Parcel Service. Parcel post includes material that does not fall into the first-, second-, or third-class categories and weighs 16 ounces or more. Rates are determined by the weight and distance the package is to be transported. Included in this category are catalogs, farm products, and miscellaneous printed matter.

Special Fourth-Class Rates include books that contain at least 24 pages and do not have advertising, 16mm (or narrower) films, educational material, printed music, loose-leaf pages and binders containing medical information, and printed test material.

Library Rates are available to libraries, schools, and nonprofit organizations.

Priority Mail includes first-class mail weighing 13 ounces or more. It is always sent by air with no guaranteed time of arrival.

Official Mail, with no postage affixed, can be sent by members of the United States Government. This includes franked mail (bearing a facsimile of the signature in the upper right corner) and penalty mail (bearing a penalty warning and "Official Business" notation).

Special Services

Special services must be transacted at the post office.

Registered Mail should be used when anything of monetary value is being sent (such as jewelry, negotiable instruments, and money); the rate charged is dependent on the amount of value declared. Registered mail must be sealed along all edges. Tape may not be used. At the time of mailing, a receipt is issued.

If the registered item is lost and a claim is properly filed, the sender can be compensated for the value declared (not to exceed $10,000), provided the sender has not and is not being reimbursed by a commercial or private insurance carrier.

Insured Mail can be insured for up to $200 and encompasses third- and fourth-class mail. If the package is lost or damaged, compensation will be made for the amount of the insurance.

Certified Mail is used when you are sending something of no monetary value; no insurance is available. The value of this type of mailing is that a return receipt can be requested, offering you proof the letter was received, to whom the letter was delivered, and the date of delivery. A slight fee is charged for each additional service.

Return Receipt for Registered, Insured and Certified Mail

UNITED STATES POSTAL SERVICE

Official Business

PENALTY FOR PRIVATE
USE, $300

Print your name, address and ZIP Code here

Jon A. Roberts
1 Bengal Lane
Salem, MA 01970

Gummed Side Pasted to the Back of the Envelope

This Side Visible

Certificates of Mailing would be used when the sender requires evidence of mailing only. The fee for this service is substantially lower than that for certified mail.

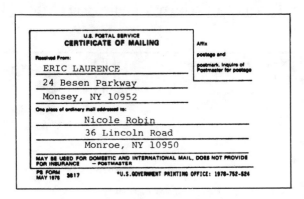

COD (Cash or Collect on Delivery) is used for first-, third-, and fourth-class mail where the addressee is responsible for payment of the postage and/or contents. The sender will receive a money order for the amount due.

Special Delivery provides the fastest delivery by messenger within certain limits of the delivery station during prescribed hours. It is available for all classes of mail.

Special Handling provides expeditious handling for third- and fourth-class mail, at a cost less than that of special delivery. This is necessary for parcels that are breakable or fragile and need special attention.

Express Mail offers a money-back guarantee that articles delivered to the post office by 5 PM will be delivered to the addressee by 3 PM the following day or can be picked up by the addressee by 10 AM the following day. Consult your local post office for additional options regarding urgent mail.

Mailgrams are transmitted via Western Union to a specific post office. The message is inserted in a window envelope and delivered by the receiving post office to the addressee.

Money Orders can be purchased and redeemed at any post

office and offer a safe and easy way to send money. Both domestic and international money orders can be purchased. The fee depends on the amount of money being transferred.

International Mail

International mail is divided into two categories:
1. LC (letters and cards), consisting of letters, letter packages, and postcards; and
2. AO (articles and others), consisting of printed matter, samples of merchandise, matter for the blind, and small packets.

When mail is directed to Mexico and Canada there is no additional charge. There are, however, higher rates and weight limits for overseas mail. Overseas packages must have a "customs declaration form" attached offering a description of the contents.

Hints for Reducing Postal Expenses

1. For certain types of mail, consider sending other than first class.
2. Keep your mailing lists up to date.
3. Presort your mail and take advantage of special presorted rates.
4. Use a postage scale, and have it checked regularly for accuracy so that you can be sure you are supplying your mail with the correct amount of postage.
5. Do not use special services unless they are necessary.
6. Obtain current postal charts.
7. Avoid using airmail for domestic mail because first-class mail is sent by air.

Special Services

Special services (such as Purolator, Federal Express and UPS) are available to expedite delivery. You can elect to have letters and packages delivered overnight, in two days, or on weekends. For more information on any of these services, call the office nearest you.

Electronic Mail (E-mail)

"Electronic mail" today provides a quick, reliable, easy and economical way to make office communications faster and more efficient. In E-mail, messages are transmitted from a computer in one location to a computer in another location. By means of a device called a modem, data from the first computer are converted into electrical impulses, which are then transmitted over ordinary telephone lines. Another modem at the other end converts the impulses back into electronic data, which are then stored in the other computer. This second computer thus acts as an "electronic mailbox" which a user can access through a simple computer program.

E-mail eliminates the office game of "telephone tag" and the perils of lost or delayed mail. Messages can be any length, the computers need not be compatible, and neither the sender nor the received has to be present for a message to be transmitted. Additionally, messages can be sent to a single address or simultaneously to hundreds of addresses—all at economical prices.

Some practical uses are:

• Marketing can send simultaneous messages to the national sales force.

- Speedy notification of production changes can enhance quality control.
- Order entry departments can coordinate delivery schedules between warehouses, etc.

CHAPTER 14

TELECOMMUNICATIONS

Telephone Services, Using the Telephone Effectively, Domestic Telegraph Services, International Telegraph Services, Facsimile (FAX) Machines, Teleconferencing

Telephone Services

DIALING INFORMATION

1. There is a slight charge for operator-assisted information calls within your calling area. Therefore, use the telephone directory provided by the telephone company. When it is necessary to contact the operator to obtain a local number, dial either 411 or 555–1212.
2. There is a charge for operator-assisted information calls outside your calling area. When such a number is needed, dial 1 + area code + 555–1212. (In some areas, the 1 is not necessary.)
3. Many organizations, in an effort to promote business, have adopted toll-free 800 numbers so that the caller will not have to pay to initiate the call. Before placing a long-distance call, always check to see if an 800 number is available. Dial 1 + 800 + 555–1212. (Again, in some areas, the 1 is not necessary.) If you call toll-free numbers

frequently, you should call or write for information about the directory available for a small charge from *The Toll-Free Digest Company*, Claverack, NY 12513.

TYPES OF SERVICES

Before placing a call outside your calling area, be certain that you have the correct area code. Also, when placing long-distance calls, be sure to calculate the difference in time zones.

Station-to-Station (direct distance dialing) calls save time and money. Place this type of call when you are willing to speak to anyone who answers. Merely dial the area code plus the number. This type of call bears the lowest rates, and charges start when the called party answers the phone.

Person-to-Person calls require operator assistance and are used when you are not certain that the called party will be available. Rates are higher than for the station-to-station calls, but there is no charge if the person you are calling is not available. Charges begin only when the called party (or extension) is connected. You dial 0 + area code + the number, and the operator comes on the line. Tell the operator that you are placing a person-to-person call and the name of the person to whom you wish to speak.

Collect calls also require operator assistance and are used when the person being called is expected to accept the charges. You dial 0 + area code + the number, and the operator comes on the line. Tell the operator you are placing a collect call. A collect call can be placed either to the number or to a particular person.

Wide-Area Telephone Service (WATS) is used by firms that make regular long-distance calls to designated areas. Access lines can be national, regional, or statewide; and rates are based on geographic area, not each call.

Mobile calls can be made to mobile units in cars, trucks,

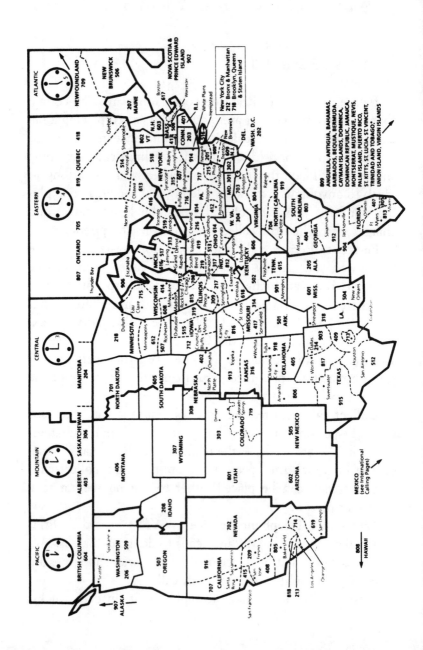

airplanes, buses, trains, and news services by contacting the mobile-service operator or by direct dialing.

Ship-to-Shore calls can be made to a person at sea by giving the long-distance operator the name of the ship, the person being called, and the number.

Conference calls can be accomplished with or without Dimension PBX equipment. You can contact the conference operator by dialing 0 and giving the operator the required numbers, names, and the time the call is to be put through. The charge for a conference call is equivalent to that of a person-to-person call for each party involved. This service can very often save the cost of travel for face-to-face meetings.

Telex provides the promptness of a telephone call and the documentation of a letter. These electromagnetic waves can be transmitted 24 hours a day, seven days a week to both domestic and international networks.

Records of times and charges are often required for accounting purposes. Many companies keep complete and accurate records of all toll calls so that the calls can be charged to the clients. Toll charges can be obtained by dialing the operator prior to placing the call and asking the operator to notify you of the toll charges after the call has been completed.

Using the Telephone Effectively

1. Speak directly into the mouthpiece in your normal voice. Your voice is magnified on the telephone, so do not shout.
2. Speak in a clear and alert manner. A flat tone can add distance between you and the listener.
3. Articulate clearly, as the listener cannot infer anything from your body language.

4. Before placing a call, you might want to jot down a few notes so that you can easily recall what you need to say.

5. Maintain a positive attitude toward the listener.

6. Say *please* and *thank you* often.

7. Use the person's name during the conversation; we all like that personal touch.

8. Try to answer by the third ring and be prepared to take a message that includes name, telephone number, message, and time of the call.

9. If a person is on hold, get back to him or her every 30 to 40 seconds so that the person will not feel forgotten.

10. Explain and apologize for long delays.

11. Be discreet about giving out information.

12. Spell any names that may be misunderstood. Clarify letters by saying "A as in apple, B as in boy," and so on.

13. Clarify numbers. For example, 16 and 60 can sound alike. Say, "Sixteen, that is, one six."

14. When placing a call, make certain you have the correct number. Keep up-to-date listings of frequently used numbers.

Telegraph Services

DOMESTIC SERVICES

Regular telegrams can be sent any time of the day or night and are usually deliverable within two hours by telephone with a written confirmation in approximately five hours. They bear a base charge for the first 10 words, with an added charge for each additional word. Regular telegrams are the most expensive form of domestic telegraph services.

Midnight telegrams can be sent until midnight and are deliverable the following morning. They bear a base charge for the first 50 words with an additional charge for each group of five words. Midnight telegrams are, therefore, recommended for more lengthy messages when there is no urgency involved.

Mailgrams are electronically wired to the post office nearest the recipient. This variation of the midnight telegram also bears a base charge for the first 50 words. The mailgram will be delivered by the mail carrier the next business day and has the advantage of conveying a sense of urgency to the recipient. Mailgrams can be sent via electronic mail service or a voice-originated telephone system.

Collect telegrams can be sent when the recipient will accept the charges.

Telex services are more fully described in the "Telephone Services" portion of this chapter.

Hotel-motel reservations and confirmations, as well as transportation tickets, are available by telegraph.

Money orders and traveler's checks can be wired to any place in the world. Payment is made by the sender and the recipient need only furnish identification to receive payment.

Candy, flowers and other special occasion items can be sent upon request.

INTERNATIONAL SERVICES

Full-rate cablegrams (FR) provide the fastest service available. They can be sent in any foreign language or code. Rates are based on the distance the message will be transmitted and bear a minimum rate for the first seven words.

Letter telegrams (LT) cannot be sent in code and are delivered the following morning, provided they are placed before midnight. There is a base charge for the first 22 words with an added charge for each additional word. The cost of this service is one-half that of the full-rate cablegram.

Telex services offer a machine-to-machine service. The fee is based on the amount of time used, not the number of words.

TELEGRAM CHARGES

Domestic
Each word, regardless of length, counted as one word
No charge for addresses or one signature

No charge for common marks of punctuation
Symbols counted as mixed group and charged accordingly

International
Each word determined on the basis of 10 letters to the word
Charge for each word in the address and the signature

Punctuation marks not allowed
Symbols (¢, #, %) must be spelled out because they cannot be transmitted in symbol form

TIPS FOR TYPING THE TELEGRAM

1. Because you are paying per word, wording should be concise and unnecessary words eliminated.

   Meet you at Kennedy Airport May 2,
   2 PM. Arriving TWA, Flight 305.

2. Type an original and two copies. The original is for Western Union, a confirmation for the addressee, and a copy for your files.

3. Single space the message using both upper and lower case letters.

4. Indicate the type of service desired and whether the message is to be sent paid, collect, or charge.

PAYMENT OF THE TELEGRAM

A telegram can be:
1. paid with cash at the time the message is sent.
2. charged to a business account.
3. charged to a telephone number.
4. charged to the recipient of the message.

Fax Machines

Fax machines are having a major impact on the way companies communicate. From a fax machine or a computer (via a network that supports fax transmissions) you can instantaneously transmit documents to any location that has a fax machine. The transmission takes place over ordinary telephone lines. The machine optically scans the document and converts the image to electronic impulses. These impulses are transmitted to the receiving unit, which converts them back into an exact copy of the original. Because a fax machine produces exact copies, you can use it to transmit not only words but also graphic images.

Teleconferencing

Teleconferencing is used in business to enable people from distant locations to "meet" without being physically together. This is expedited by video cameras, microphones, television monitors, and FAX equipment. It has the advantage of enabling people to engage in personal contact without necessitating the time and expense of travel.

- *Audio conferencing* (voice only) between two people in remote locations is aided by the use of extension phones. Additional sites can be included by means of an electronic device called a bridge. Telephones can be purchased with built-in bridges. The bridges help to equalize volume on each telephone and participants can dial into a conference in any location.
- *Video conferencing* (visual transmission) utilizes cameras, monitors, and projection equipment. Still pictures allow transmission of anything the camera is aimed at, while full-motion video requires the same kind of high-capacity transmission lines used by commercial television networks.
- *Computer conferencing* allows participants with computer terminals to call up from computer memory documents, graphics, and so on, and transmit them from one terminal to another. In order for terminals to communicate, a modem and communications software are required.

CHAPTER 15

RECORDS MANAGEMENT

Alphabetic Filing, Numerical Filing, Geographic Filing, Subject Filing, Tips for Locating Misplaced Files

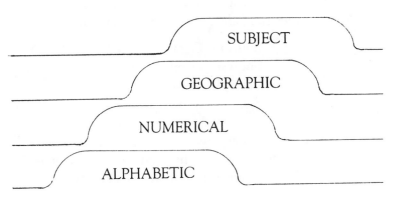

If you have ever used the telephone directory, you have applied records management principles. The white pages are arranged in alphabetical order; the pages themselves, in numerical order; the yellow pages, by subject; and each directory, by geographic location.

Uniformity in filing is essential because the filing and instant retrieval of records is the backbone of any organization. The system used must be understood by all who have need for the records.

Alphabetic Filing

NAMES OF INDIVIDUALS

1. To prepare a personal name for filing, place in proper indexing order: surname, first name, middle name or initial.

   > Sullivan, Thomas Ira

2. Alphabetize names by comparing each unit letter by letter. When names have the same first units,* alphabetize according to the second unit, and so on. A standard rule to remember is: *Nothing comes before something.*

   > Sullivan, Gerald
   > Sullivan, Gerald A.
   > Sullivan, Lynne Mary
   > Sullivan, Robyn M.

3. A prefix to a surname (such as *Mc, Mac, d, de, Van, O',* *St.*) is considered part of the name and not a separate unit. *St.* is alphabetized as if it were spelled out, *Saint.*

   > d'Angeli, Josephine Carla
   > Dangeli, Rita B.
   > St. James, James C.
   > Saint Thomas, William

4. A hyphenated name is considered a single unit and is treated as one name.

Units refers to the sections, or parts, of a name. For example, in *Sullivan, Gerald A.*, *Sullivan* is the first unit; *Gerald*, the second; and A., the third.

> Harwood, Laura-Beth
> Johns-Allen, Michael

5. Titles, seniority terms, and other designations are dropped from the end of the name for filing purposes. When a married woman's first name is known, use it. When unknown, she is listed as surname, husband's name, *Mrs.*, to distinguish her from her husband.

> Bergstein, Susan
> Bergstein, Warren Mrs.

NAMES OF BUSINESSES AND ORGANIZATIONS

6. Each word of a firm name is treated as a separate unit. When the firm name, however, includes the surname and first name of an individual, transpose the parts of the individual's name.

> Teisch, Morton, Consultant Co.
> Reda Pharmacy, Inc.

7. Articles, conjunctions, and prepositions in English are disregarded for filing purposes. Foreign articles, such as *El*, *La*, *Les*, *Thy*, are included.

> La Pluma Cafe
> (The) Specialty Pastry Shoppe

8. Abbreviations are filed as if written out.

> Geiger Lumber Co.
> Geiger Lumber Company, Inc.

9. Single letters in a name are treated as separate units when they are not known abbreviations.

> ABC Chemical Company
> XYZ Electronics, Inc.

10. Hyphenated firm names are treated as one unit.

> A-B Chemical Company
> Marshall-Dylan Department Store

11. When two names of a business firm can be properly written as one, treat as a single unit.

> Inter National Antiques, Ltd.
> International Jewelry Exchange

12. Numbers in a business firm are filed as if written out and treated as a single unit.

> Eighteen hundred House
> Seven Brothers Associates

13. Compound geographic names are treated as separate units with the exception of *San*, *Los*, and other short foreign names.

> San Francisco Realty Company
> Santa Clara Antiques

14. Banks, hospitals, and religious institutions are listed in the order written.

> Good Samaritan Hospital
> Union State Bank

NAMES OF DOMESTIC AND FOREIGN
GOVERNMENTS

15. Branches of the U.S. Government are filed with *U.S. Government* as the first three units. Then comes the department, bureau, division, commission, etc., with the distinctive name of the department considered first.

> U.S. Government, Interior Department
> U.S. Government, Internal Revenue Service

16. State and local governments are filed according to the distinctive name followed by the state, city, etc. Then comes the department, bureau, division, commission, etc. As above, the distinctive part of the department is filed first.

> New Jersey State, Education Department
> New York State, Regents Board

17. To index foreign governments, consider the dominion, kingdom, etc. first followed by the name of the country. Then proceed as you would with domestic governments.

> Denmark, Kingdom, State Department
> Germany, Federal Republic, State Department

Numerical Filing

Numerical filing, the arrangement of records according to numbers, has the following advantages:

1. Names can be identical; numbers cannot.
2. Files can be expanded more easily because you can add

storage units as necessary. In the other filing systems, it may be necessary to rearrange complete files as drawers become too crowded.

3. Confidentiality is increased because numbers are impersonal in nature.

4. Many systems make use of numbers already in use, such as social security numbers, telephone numbers, and account numbers.

Numerical filing is managed in three different ways:

CONSECUTIVE NUMBER FILING

This system is used primarily when the identifying numbers contain no more than four digits. The numbers are read from left to right with higher numbers filed behind lower ones.

1234
1235
1236

MIDDLE DIGIT FILING

This system is primarily used when numbers are grouped in three units. The group in the middle is considered the first unit (1); the group on the left, the second unit (2); and the group on the right, the third unit (3). Note: Although you are sequencing according to the middle digits, do not change the order of the numbers.

2	1	3
06	15	791
07	15	158
56	26	730
01	28	033

TERMINAL DIGIT FILING

This system is primarily used when numbers are grouped in units. The group to the right is the first unit and the units are thereafter read from right to left.

3	2	1
01	28	033
07	15	158
56	26	730
06	15	791

Geographic Filing

Geographic filing, the arrangement of records according to location, is used when this is the most efficient means for a company. Sales organization and manufacturers employ this system to indicate domestic and/or international territories and utility companies use it to indicate customer locations.

An international system categorizes according to the name of the country; a domestic system categorizes according to the name of the state. Following the state, the city is considered, and then the name of the company.

New York, Albany, James & Sons, Inc.
New York, Albany, Zone Planning Enterprises
New York, Buffalo, A & S Stationery Supplies
Virginia, Richmond, Local Contractors, Inc.
Virginia, Suffolk, AAA Auto Supplies
    Company

Subject Filing

Subject filing, the arrangement of records according to topics, is used when it is expedient for a company to file according to topics such as items, objects, business activities, and functions.

The sequencing of these files is like that found in the yellow pages of your telephone directory.

Physicians	Leon Andersen, M.D.
	Michael Cavanagh, M.D.
	Isadore Sternlieb, M.D.
Schools	Elmwood Elementary School
	Spring Valley Junior High School
	Spring Valley Senior High School

Tips for Locating Misplaced Paper Files

1. Look on your employer's desk and in his/her briefcase, and ask others who use the file.
2. Look in the file folder in front of and in back of the missing one. It might have been placed inadvertently in one of these folders.
3. If your office uses an alphabetic filing system, look under various spellings of the name. In a numerical filing system, look under various numerical arrangements. In a geographic filing system, look under the same or similar names in other cities and/or states. For a lost file in a subject filing system, look under related headings. For *janitorial services*, for instance, look under *maintenance*.

Records Management Technology

AUTOMATED RECORDS SYSTEMS

An automated system refers to one that uses an electronic computer to process and store information. There is a great emphasis in today's office to minimize the proliferation of paperwork via computerization and the electronic storage of records. We have often heard the "modern office" referred to as the *paperless office*. However unlikely that may really be, there are many types of computer storage files that are helping to move us in the direction of the *paperless office*. Examples include the following:

- *Magnetic tape*—Film-like rolls of tape storing records in binary code. The cost is very low and little storage space is needed, but you cannot read an isolated file without first reading all preceding files.
- *Magnetic disk*—Cylinder-like in appearance storing records on circular tracks much like a jukebox arrangement of phonograph records. As opposed to magnetic tape, you can access a file directly without going through all preceding files, but storage costs are higher.

MICROGRAPHICS

A variety of micrographics is also available in response to the wide variety of applications and needs of today's office. Micrographics must be stored in an environment free of dust, moisture, and extreme temperature changes.

- *Microfilm* is similar to movie film, storing a series of pictures.

- *Microfiche* (or fiche) is a sheet of film containing microimages. Although the size can vary, four by six inches is the most common.
- *Ultrafiche* is similar to micfiche but it can store thousands of images.
- *Aperture cards* are standard eighty-column punched cards prepared on a keypunch machine.

NOTE: Special equipment is needed to prepare micrographics and to read micrographics.

COMPUTER DATA BANKS

A collection of data bases (sources of information) offers the user instant access to a wide variety of information. In order to access a data base (for a fee, of course) you must have a modem, giving you the ability to communicate. You can have a library of information at your fingertips offering information on banking, biographies, computers, dissertations, economics, encyclopedias, finance, government, inventions, law, medicine, newspapers, patents, publishing, sports, transportation, and so on.

CHAPTER 16

PROOFREADING
AND EDITING

Quality control is a term that has been bandied about often. It has been related to the automobile industry, to the high-technology industry, and to most industries where products are manufactured for consumer use. Quality control means controlling the quality of the items being presented so that they are free from defects. Have you ever purchased a new automobile only to have a knob fall off or to hear a rattle?

As a proofreader, YOU control the quality of the paperwork being generated by seeing that it has met the basic business standards in terms of appearance and technical output. Proofreading and editing are not innate talents; they are skills—skills that can be learned and developed.

Each document should be carefully proofread several times checking for:

- formatting
- styling
- English usage
- word repetition
- omissions
- spacing
- transpositions
- hyphenations

- names and addresses
- numbers
- spelling
- general sense of the text

Some factors to keep in mind when proofreading and editing are:

1. Scan the overall text to make certain that the format and style are correct.
2. Accurately pinpoint any typographical errors, punctuation errors, and/or grammatical errors.
3. Double-check the spelling of all names, initials, and any statistical information.
4. Pay special attention to small words (as, in, an, and, it, if) that are often overlooked.
5. Pay special attention also to homonyms (*their* and *there*, *its* and *it's*). Many word-processing programs feature a spelling check; however, no spelling check can differentiate between homonyms.
6. Check the continuity of all numbered pages, paragraphs, and exercises.
7. Spelling can be double-checked by reading the text from bottom to top or right to left, concentrating on each individual word.
8. When revising text on a word processor, you need only to proofread the portion of the text that has been changed because (assuming you proofread accurately the first time) only the portion you changed has been altered.
9. If you are proofreading technical or statistical data, the "buddy system" is recommended when another person is available. Give a copy of your typewritten text to the other person and read from the original copy. Carefully pronounce all word endings (s, ed, ing) and spell out any unusually spelled names.

10. If you are proofreading technical or statistical data and there is no one who can assist you, place the information side by side and follow line by line with a straightedge (ruler or envelope).

Computers have greatly simplified the process of proofreading. Many software programs come with a built-in spelling checker that can search for words it doesn't recognize, double words, words with numbers, capitalization errors, etc.

Many programs also come with a built-in thesaurus that will display synonyms and antonyms. And there are even programs that will check grammar.

Proofreader's Marks

Very often, you will be creating a draft that you know will need revisions. Once an error has been detected, you must be able to communicate the necessary changes in a standardized method. Such a method is through the use of proofreader's marks. Proofreader's marks must be neat and accurate so that anyone viewing the text will understand your intentions.

∽ transpose	to completely finish or abⁿʳᵗᵒᵗ
∧ insert	we would᷊ᴸⁱᵏᵉ to have your input
ꝑ delete	in our ouͬ judgment
⌒ close space	ear͜ache
⌒/ delete and close space	it is our con͜ᵗcern

⌐#	leave space	stomach⌐ache
stet	retain deleted material	the President has ~~asked~~ ⌐ stet
lc	lower case (small letter)	their Åccounting Ɗepartment
≡	upper case (capital letter)	Star wars or <u>Star Wars</u>
ss	single space	We would like to ss have your opinion of ss what transpired
os	double space	os We would like to have your opinion of os what transpired
TS	triple space	TS We would like to have your opinion of TS what transpired
⧸⧸⧸	remove underscore	a <u>very</u> well-known man
◯	spell out fully	(Fed.)
⌐#⌐	indent (# of spaces)	5 Now is the time
¶	new paragraph	we have been.¶ This would be

Symbol	Meaning	Example
no ¶	no new paragraph	*no* ¶ This would have been
→ ←	center on page	→ TOTALS ←
∼∼	boldface type	WHO AND WHOM
∫	reverse order	pencils and paper / staples and staplers
∀	apostrophe	men's department
⊙	colon	the following ⊙
⌃	comma	If you will please
⌃	semicolon	New York, New York Trenton
x x	ellipsis	Now is the x x x
(!)	exclamation point	Alas (!)
∧	hyphen	well trained staff
⊙	period	as well ⊙
" "	quotation marks	The Good Life
⌐ ⌐	move up	The Trials of Time
⌊ ⌋	move down	The Great Deception
⊏	move to the left	⊏ this is the one

⌐ move to the right   ⌐ this is the one

// align type   // We are in the
                                midst of a very
                                important

⟨?⟩ Verify information or   on May 6⟨?⟩we were
    add question mark

ital italicize   Safe at Any *ital*

— underscore   <u>Words</u>

Part III.
Electronic
Office
Technology

CHAPTER 17

WORD PROCESSING

Word Processing Equipment, Word Processing Terms

The term *word processing* can apply to any method of transferring ideas and information into written documents. It normally means using electronic equipment to generate, edit, store, transmit, and duplicate documents. Word processing equipment has made all these processes far more efficient.

Word Processing Equipment

A vast array of word processors and computers has flooded the market, ranging from simple to complex. Regardless of the complexity, however, all hardware (equipment) bears the same components: keyboard, central processing unit (CPU), disk drive, display, and printer.

The following is an explanation of the various components:

KEYBOARD

The placement of alphabetic and numeric keys is *standard* and conforms to any typewriter keyboard. Additional function

laser printer

display

CPU

disk drive

mouse

keyboard

Courtesy of International Business Machines Corporation

keys (varying from one machine to another) enable you to perform specific tasks quickly and easily. Once you have learned the electronic keyboard, transferring from one machine to another will not be difficult because the similarities far outweigh the differences. Many keyboards have an additional ten-key pad (similar to a calculator) for faster numeric entry.

CENTRAL PROCESSING UNIT

The central processing unit (CPU), also known as the terminal or computer, is the "brains" of the unit that receives commands from the keyboard. It serves as the central location for the storage and distribution of data.

You will be hearing numbers such as 640K or 4MB, and so on. "K" refers to the per thousand internal memory capabilities that can be stored in the memory of the computer. "MB" refers to megabytes.

DISK DRIVE

The disk drive functions in much the same way as a tape recorder with "read" and "write" heads. A floppy disk/diskette is inserted into the drive for recording text and communicating instructions to the CPU.

A *hard drive* is used to store and retrieve. Floppy disks are used for backups and copies of files.

DISPLAY

The display, also known as monitor, cathode ray tube (CRT) or video display terminal (VDT), is basically a TV-like screen that displays the text. It enables you to view a document for editing, thereby producing error-free final copy. Displays are available in full color or in monochrome combinations of green on black, white on black, white on green, or amber on black.

PRINTER

Computer printers can be one of several types.

- *Dot matrix printers* produce small dots that form characters and/or shapes.
- *Laser printers* offer the ultimate in speed and quality. They utilize a laser beam that burns characters onto light-sensitive paper to give a typeset look.

MODEM

A modem is a device that gives you the ability to communicate with other computers. It connects with ordinary telephone lines, which carry information in the form of electronic impulses to or from users at other locations.

SOFTWARE

In order to carry out any word processing assignment, you must have software. Software is a preprogrammed set of instructions on diskette(s) that give your computer added capabilities.

A wide variety of software packages are available that will allow you to do basic word processing, page layout, graphic illustration, spreadsheets, and database management.

Each software package comes with a user manual that will give you instructions on how to use each of its features. It is to your advantage to keep the user manual handy and USE IT.

DISKETTES

Diskettes are known as disks, floppy disks, or floppy diskettes. In addition to containing software programs, diskettes are used to store your data. Diskettes come in two sizes: 5.25" and 3.5".

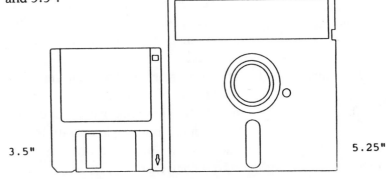

3.5"   5.25"

CARING FOR YOUR DISKETTES

The 5.25" floppy diskettes are more vulnerable than the 3.5" because they don't have a hard shell.

- Keep them in their envelopes when they're not being used.
- Don't bend them.
- Never touch the film that you can see through the elongated opening at the bottom.
- Don't write on the label with anything other than a soft marker.

For both size diskettes:

- Keep them away from bright sunlight.
- Keep them away from any magnetic forces.
- Store them at temperatures from 50°F to 125°F or 10°C to 50°C.

Word Processing Terms

alphanumeric
: a combination of alphabetic and numerical characters

automatic equipment
: equipment that performs many tasks such as centering, carriage return, line spacing, and centering either automatically or by key-stroke command

basic document cycle
: creation, storage, use, transfer, and disposal of a record

batch
: a collection of similar work that can be produced in a single operation

bit
: the smallest unit of information

boot
: start a computer

byte
: a sequence of bits, usually shorter than a word

character
: a letter, number, or symbol

cluster
: a work group or unit of employees and/or equipment

COM
: computer output microfilm

command
: instruction to the computer to perform a certain function

communicating typewriter
: equipment that can send and receive information with another communicating typewriter via telephone hookups

CPS
: characters per second

CPU
: central processing unit

crash
: disk down (inoperable)

CRT
: cathode ray tube, a TV-like screen for the display of characters

cursor
: a movable indicator on a CRT which indicates the place for editing a document

database	files of information used by an organization
debug	remove errors ("bugs") from a software program
delete	instruction to remove text from a document
desktop publishing	using the computer to generate text and/or graphics of "publishable" quality
directory	a list of documents
discrete media	belts, disks, cartridges, and cassettes that are removable for storage
disk (or diskette or disc)	computer equipment used for recording, transcribing, and storing data
document	a file (letter, report, etc.)
down	equipment inoperable
edit	to revise a text
element	a removable, replaceable printer
endless loop	a sealed, continuous loop inside a tank that allows for simultaneous dictating and transcribing
facsimile (FAX)	the transmission and reception of textual copy through telephone lines
field	a unit of similar information

Example: Name [   ]

Phone [   ]

floppy disk	a pliable type of disk
font	an assortment of characters in one type size and style
hard copy	typed or printed texts
hardware	word processing equipment

hot zone	the area in which editing equipment will determine where the right-hand margin should be
ink jet printer	a printing device that electronically squirts ink onto paper in character form
input	information entered into a system for processing
I/O	input/output device
IWPA	International Word Processing Association, an association that deals with systems and methods of word processing
justification	the position of the characters in relation to the left and right margins.
menu	selection of options
mouse	a small, hand-held device that can substitute for many computer commands by clicking the buttons and dragging the mouse
OCR	optical character recognition
off-line	equipment not connected to or dependent on peripheral equipment
on-line	equipment connected to and dependent on peripheral equipment
output	the final results produced
PBX	private branch exchange (telephone system)
peripheral equipment	equipment that works with the central unit, such as keyboards and printers
procedures manual	a manual that gives the step-by-step process for completing a certain task
RAM	(Random Access Memory) The most common temporary storage memory
reprographics	reproduction of a document

ROM	(Read Only Memory) Permanent storage on the computer.
search	a command given to locate previously recorded information
shared logic	a system that allows two or more units to utilize the memory of a single CPU
software	programs and routines needed to use hardware
stand-alone unit	a self-contained, independent unit
station	the work location for a WP operator
store	to place in memory information not subject to change
terminal	a device that can send and receive information
text-editing equipment	a WP typewriter capable of revising texts
time-sharing	the simultaneous use of the CPU
turnaround time	the time that elapses from the beginning to the completion of a task
variable	a segment of a document subject to change
VOR	voice operated relay, a device that activates a recorder when it senses that a voice is coming over the line

CHAPTER 18

DESKTOP PUBLISHING

Project Planning, Page Layout, Type, Graphics, Printing, DTP Terms

Desktop Publishing (DTP) has created perhaps the most dramatic change in today's office insofar as the way we present ideas. The secretary who knows DTP is considered a highly skilled specialist who can command a higher salary than his/her non-DTP counterparts.

WHAT EXACTLY IS DESKTOP PUBLISHING?

DTP is much more than word processing; it's actually creating letterhead, brochures, newsletters, flyers, advertisements, forms, manuals, etc., right from your computer. You can generate professional-quality pages using special software that offers typesetting, graphics and page make-up functions. Laser printed pages can be used either as finished copy or as camera-ready copy for a professional printer.

In days of yore (pre-DTP), after you created a manuscript, you would send it out for typesetting, proofreading, revisions, paste-up, and then send the finished document to a printer. If there were last minute changes, you'd have to make the corrections, send them back to the typesetter, go through more rounds of proofreading, repaste the graphics, and then send the document to the printer. This process could go on ad nauseam and would often result in major time delays and additional expenses.

In a DTP environment, you have control over the entire production process because, essentially, you have your own publishing system.

It is the intention of this chapter to acquaint you with some of the many DTP capabilities, not to teach you design skills or how to use any particular DTP software.

Project Planning

Always work with a schedule. It is helpful to schedule backwards from the date the finished product is due; this allows you to plan the maximum time for each step. Try to create a tighter schedule than you think you'll need in order to allow for the unexpected. Last minute changes are a fact of life. People who aren't involved in DTP don't always realize how "just one little change" can effect an entire project. One word can completely alter the page flow, effecting the placement of graphics, the table of contents, the index, etc.

Prepare a written schedule that includes all the steps involved, the scheduled date of each step, the actual date that each step was completed, and a place for comments. Give a copy of the schedule to all the people involved in the project. If you find you're falling behind schedule due to factors beyond your control, it might be a good idea to meet with the people involved in order to adjust the schedule or determine how some time can be made up.

This chapter is devoted to specific areas of DTP:

- Page layout
- Type

- Graphics
- Printing

DPT terms are included at the end of this chapter.

Page Layout

The page layout should achieve two purposes:

- Draw attention to the printed piece
- Establish order

In doing so, the design should create pages that are pleasing to the eye and easy to read.

MASTER PAGE LAYOUT

The first step in preparing a master page layout is determining the common design elements that will carry through the publication. Most page-layout programs will ask you to indicate:

- page size (8½" × 11", 5½" × 8", etc.)
- top and bottom margins
- inside and outside margins
- number of columns
- space between columns (gutters)
- number of rows
- space between rows
- facing pages
- headers and footers, if any
- placement of page number

The following is an example of single-column, facing pages.

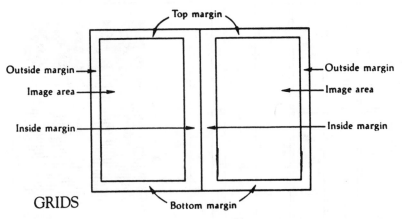

GRIDS

A well-designed document will display structure, giving the reader a sense of familiarity, continuity, and comfort—but still offer the flexibility to deviate for special effect.

There are no rigid rules to using grids. Think about the type of project you're doing and the impact on the reader. Grids can have as few as one or two columns or as many as seven or eight. The following are some guidelines:

No. of Columns	Appropriate for
1, 2, or 3	Reports, manuals and proposals
4	Tabloids or many visuals to work into a two-column layout
5	Two-column layout where a narrow column is used for headlines, subheadlines, quotes, etc.
6	Two- or three-column newsletters where there will be several visuals or interesting column structure
7 or 8	Creative layouts

Notice how the same five-column grid can be used for a number of different layouts using the same text and graphics.

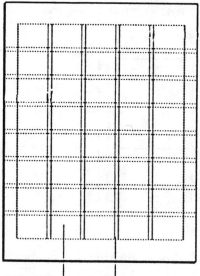

Grid unit |

Gutter |

Page Layout Hints

- Plan for white space. White space will shape and frame the content and will present an elegant, and appealing piece.
- Use more than one color, if your budget will allow. If not, shading is an effective styling tool.
- Include borders, boxes, oversized page numbers, etc. for added eye appeal. But don't clutter your page.

Type

SIZE

Type size is measured in points; the larger the point size, the larger the type.

8 point

10 point

12 point

14 point

18 point

24 point

CLASSIFICATIONS

Typefaces fall into two basic categories: serif and sans serif.

Serif

Sans Serif

- *Serifs* are the little strokes at the end of the letters. Serifs are generally used for blocks of text because they act as cues to guide the reader's eye horizontally. Most books are printed in serif for that reason. Popular serif fonts are Times, Garamond, Cheltenham and Palatino.
- *Sans serif* means without serifs, from the French word *sans* (without). Sans serifs are clean and crisp and are often used for posters, scientific materials, call-outs, or directories. Popular sans serif fonts are Helvetica, Avant Garde and Optima.

MIXING TYPEFACES

Conventional wisdom says, don't go overboard mixing type-faces because not all are compatible. If you stay with one or two typefaces, you will ensure visual compatibility. Many publications use serif for the text and sans serif for headlines. Times Roman (serif) and Helvetica (sans serif) are the two most frequently used typefaces.

EMPHASIZING TEXT

There are several ways to emphasize text, but moderation is the key. Here are some guidelines:

- ALL CAPS: Reserve this emphasis for very strong words such as IMPORTANT or WARNING. You may want to try small caps, if they're available.
- *Italics:* This can be tedious and difficult to read, so use it only to emphasize phrases.
- **Boldface:** Good for headlines or for entire paragraphs that need to be emphasized.
- Underscore: Try boldface or italics instead. Underscoring was popular in the days of the typewriter because options were limited. Underscoring tends to cut through the descenders, making the text difficult to read.

LEADING

Leading (pronounced ledding) is the space added between lines of type and is measured from one baseline of text to the next baseline.

> This is 10-point Dutch type with a
> 10-point leading. It is called "10/10"
> (10 on 10).

> This is 10-point Dutch type with a
> 12-point leading. It is called "10/12"
> (10 on 12).

TYPE HINTS

Desktop publishing has typing style rules that may be somewhat different from those of the typewriter because typewriters are more limited in their capabilities. Here are some general typing style rules for desktop publishing:

- Use only one space after a period, not two. DTP systems offer proportional spacing. Typewriters offer only monospacing.
  Examples:
  This is an example of monospacing. Each character is the same width.
  This is an example of proportional spacing—different widths for different characters.
- Use an em-dash rather than two hyphens. An em-dash is a thin line about the width of the letter m.
- Use correct quotation marks, those that are "curly." What appears on your keyboard is actually an inch mark. This also applies to apostrophes.
- If you're writing foreign words or phrases, use the proper accents or diacritical marks.

mañana　　　　　résumé
garçon　　　　　Götterdämmerung

- Use the special character set to generate symbols, fractions, etc.

← →	arrows	®	registration
100°	degrees	©	copyright
÷	divided into	™	trademark
±	plus or minus	℞	Rx
⅝	fraction	♫	sixteenth note
π	pi	Σ	SIGMA

- Avoid widows (individual lines of type carried over to the top of the next page) and orphans (individual lines of type that remain on the preceding page).
- Don't justify columns that are too narrow or you'll wind up with rivers of white space cascading down the page.
- Avoid headlines with two or more lines of equal length. Try to achieve a rag right.
- The first paragraph of a publication is generally flush left, especially when the headline is centered.

Graphics

The human mind processes visual images faster than written words, and visuals are retained 65% longer. Therefore, graphics that are used appropriately will command the readers' attention. You don't have to be a Michelangelo to turn out high-quality graphics.

ELECTRONIC CLIP ART

Electronic clip art is a collection of drawings and illustrations that can be used to enhance presentations, reports, proposals, newsletters, memos, or any written communications. Electronic clip art is public domain and copyright free.

The following are some of the many electronic clip art illustrations that are available.

BOX IT

Something as simple as drawing a box around text can effectively draw attention to a specific paragraph or section.

Shadow Box

Double Box

GRAPHS AND CHARTS

Graphs and charts also make excellent visuals and there are software programs to help you prepare them.

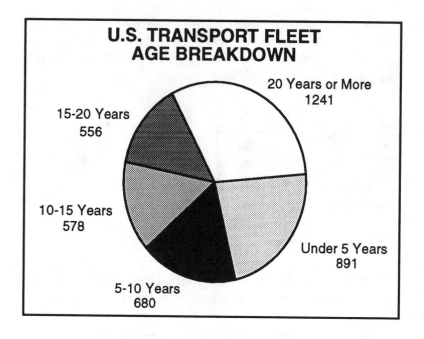

DRAWING AND PAINT PROGRAMS

Drawing and paint programs allow you to create illustrations to be used with your page-layout program. Drawing programs are generally used for simple geometrical shapes, mechanical drawings, or any illustration where you need to connect point A to point B. Paint programs are somewhat more complicated and are generally used by artists and illustrators. The images created by drawing and paint applications can be transported into a page-layout program and cropped, enlarged or reduced to fit into your text.

SCANNING

A scanner is a machine that converts hard copy images into computer-usable form. Scanning opens up many graphic possibilities, allowing you to capture anything from a line image to a color or black-and-white photograph. In order to scan, you'll need a scanner that is compatible with your drawing and page-layout program.

Printing

The decision to use a laser printer, a quick print shop, a conventional offset print shop, or a web printer will be determined by the quality you require, the type of project, and the budget.

- **Laser printers** offer good quality in black and white or color. There is special laser paper that will give you the highest possible quality. However, you are limited by the toner cartridges, the available fonts, and the low resolution (usually 300 dots per inch). You're also limited by the paper size and the slowness of producing multiple copies. A laser printer will often be used to produce camera-ready copy to be turned over to a conventional print shop.
- **Quick print shops** are often identifiable by "insta-," "quick-," or "speedy" in the name. These shops often use paper printing plates without film negatives. If your job has heavy ink coverage or fine lines, you may be sacrificing some quality. And don't be fooled by the words "speedy" or "quick"; this isn't always so.
- **Conventional offset print shops** are offset printers that offer professional quality, large print runs, four-color print processes, and the highest halftone quality.
- **Web printers** specialize in roll-fed paper rather than sheet-fed paper. Your paper choices are generally limited. This is a perfect application for newspapers, telephone directories, etc.

ASSEMBLY SHEETS

The printer needs to know what appears on each page, even if a page is blank. It's important to keep the continuity of right-hand pages (having odd numbers) and left-hand pages (having even numbers). It's also critical that figures, tables, and illustrations are placed according to your instructions. There are two ways of insuring this:

1. Prepare a dummy of the entire document, which is an exact representation of the finished product.
2. Prepare an assembly sheet, which is a line-by-line listing of exactly what appears on each page.

FOLDING

When printing a large publication, such as a book or pamphlet, pages aren't printed individually. Instead a signature is prepared. A signature is a large single sheet that is folded into increments of four. The signature is then trimmed to create individual pages.

The following is an example of a 16-page signature and how several signatures are assembled to create a book.

16-page signature folded

folded signatures gathered

folded and gathered signatures
ready for binding

BINDING

After the signatures have been assembled and trimmed, they're sent to the bindery. Some examples of binding techniques and their possible applications include:

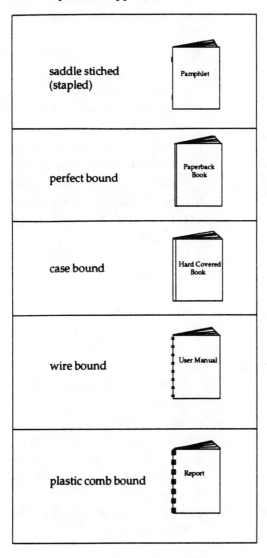

Desktop Publishing Terms

AAs	author's alterations
alley	unprinted area between columns
ascender	part of a letter which rises above the main body
autoflow	text which flows continuously onto successive pages
binding	process that holds the document together
bleed	printed image in which the ink has been printed right to the edge of the page
blueline (or blues)	photoprint made from a stripped-up negative—used as a final proof
boldface	type that is heavier than the text type
bulk	degree of thickness of the paper
camera-ready	exact material to be photographed and printed
caption	a block of words describing a photo or illustration
clip art	public domain art that can be used as is or customized
coated paper	paper with a coating to give it either a glossy or dull finish
color separation	process of separating full-color originals into the four primary color printing groups
comp	comprehensive (see dummy)
copy	text portion of the manuscript
crop	edit or cut a portion of a photograph
crop marks	lines that indicate where the page should be trimmed
descender	part of a letter which extends below the main body

dingbats	decorative characters such as asterisks, circles, check marks, etc.
drilling	punching holes in paper to permit insertion into a ringed binder
dummy	preliminary layout showing the position of the text and graphics
facing pages	double-sized, even- and odd-numbered pages that face each other
folio	page number
font	assortment of characters for each size and style of typeface
footer	element that will appear on the bottom of all designated pages
format	size, style, typeface, page size, margins, and printing requirements of a document
four-color process	printing technique using the four primary colors of ink
galleys	long sheets of photographic paper which can be cut and pasted onto finished pages
greeking	simulating the document using Latin or nonsense text where the actual text will appear
grid	system of vertical and horizontal lines divided into rectangular patterns, used to position text and graphics on a page
gutter	see alley
hairline rule	very thin line
halftone	reproduction of artwork that converts the image into dots of various sizes
header	element that will appear at the top of all designated pages
hickey	spots or imperfections on a page

indicia	mailing information required by the post office as a substitute for a stamp
kerning	adjusting horizontal spaces between the letters to make them aesthetically pleasing
landscape	orientation where text is horizontal (wider than tall)
leading	(pronounced ledding) amount of vertical spacing between the tops of the upper case letters in two successive lines of text
master page	guide for other pages in the text
matte paper	dull-finished paper
measure	width of a line of type, usually expressed in picas
mechanical	camera-ready copy (also known as paste-up)
offset printing	an inked image on a flat plate that is transferred to a rubber surface before being pressed on paper
overlay	transparent covering placed as protection over artwork
perfect binding	the process of gluing pages to the spine (as in a book)
pica	printers unit of measurement (6 picas = 1 inch)
pixels	dots on your screen that form images
point	unit of measurement to specify type sizes
portrait	orientation where text is vertical (taller than wide)
press run	number of printed impressions specified for production
proof	sample copy against which the original is checked
ragged (rag)	leaving one side of a column unjustified

registration marks	markings that show a commercial printer where to trim the finished page
relief	projection of letters or images from a flat surface
resolution	clarity of detail
reverse type	white text on a colored or shaded background
rules	lines added to a page to enhance the style or readability
saddle stitched	binding that places staples through the middle fold of collated sheets
sans serif	typeface without serifs
scanner	device that reads text or graphics and converts it into a computerized image
score	impression (dent) for easier folding
self-cover	cover with paper stock the same as the inside pages
self-mailer	a printed piece that can be mailed without an envelope
serif	lines that finish the main strokes of a letter
shrink wrap	materials packaged in a tightly sealed transparent outer wrapping
signature	large single printed sheet, in multiples of four, that is folded into page sizes
template	(see grid)
thumbnail	small sketch of a page
tint	percentage of shading
weight	thickness or heaviness of paper
white space	planned areas of empty space
WYSIWYG	(What You See Is What You Get) describes a system that displays on the screen exactly how the printed page will look